DEDICATION

To my mother and father,
From whom I learned perseverance.

TABLE OF CONTENTS

THE SMALL BUSINESS SURVIVAL *Guide*

Insights into the First Two Years

By Alrick A. Robinson

ISBN: 1439268312
ISBN-13: 9781439268315

PREFACE

IT IS YOUR ATTITUDE, NOT YOUR APTITUDE, THAT DETERMINES YOUR ALTITUDE.

President Obama frequently reminds us that we are facing the worst recession since the Great Depression. That might be so. But it is our collective attitude that got us here.

Paradoxically, people have more information, are better educated, and are more informed than before, but our negative attitudes brought us to this crisis, and it is a change in attitude that will get us out of the hole.

I browsed through a book about starting your own business, and it specifically mentioned people in their adventurous twenties. The author said that most people over the age of twenty-one dream of starting their own business and probably most who take the plunge never turn back.

Not true.

Traditionally, most businesses fail within two years or so. Some might seem to be "successful" but struggle to get ahead and soon fold. Some are, in fact, subsidized by their owners.

The reasons for this struggle are many and varied, but make no mistake: a business takes on its own personality and requires an approach to its life and livelihood similar to any other notable pursuit of progress and success. But do the statistics have to be so grim?

I have formed a number of businesses, including a couple that did not make it beyond a few months. One has been around for over twelve years. I plan to start others and am very prepared for the odds. I want to pass on the challenges I have encountered, plus the observations of others, to help make life easier for those who have the guts to start their own businesses.

The ideas presented in this book are not "new" in the sense that they are unheard of. They are the products of common sense and experience. My willingness to observe and learn from failures and successes allowed these ideas to fall into place and provide some valuable lessons. The right attitude, when applied to challenging situations, will improve one's chances of success significantly.

ACKNOWLEDGMENTS

I cannot easily list the many persons who made this book possible. My son Gregory provided invaluable computer skills and helped me with gusto. My son Brandon was encouraging, and my wife, Audrey, has always had confidence in my abilities, which she extended to this, another of my projects. But special thanks and appreciation go to the persons who unknowingly provided the book's foundation through their challenges and answers over the years.

At first, the many issues did not seem to provide anything other than a source of frustration and difficulty, but as things evolved, the lessons became priceless! They came from interactions with employees, customers, prospects, competitors, suppliers, colleagues, and virtually every area of business.

The insights through my growing awareness have been shared with the hope of uplifting others as I have been uplifted.

INTRODUCTION

When I consider how many books about starting a business have been written that are considered "good" because of their style, content, or relevance, I am amazed at how rarely they are put to practical use. This fact fascinates me because one cannot deny that information is given. Extrapolate that to courses and seminars and you get similar results. The success rate of the material presented is not very high because there is a mental aspect that creates a block of some sort. You read and "feel good," but the doing gets left behind.

Take planning. There are well-respected teachers and coaches who send me (among others) frequent information on planning. This is most prevalent at or about the end of the year and at the start of a new year. They implore me to set goals and to have different types—life goals, personal goals, business goals, relationship goals, financial goals, and so on. Then there are the timelines—five-year plans, broken down into one-year plans, then into months and weeks. They promise bonuses for signing up for their services, and they cite testimonials from those who, supposedly, have finally gotten their lives sorted out after subscribing.

Well, the truth is that very few people actually apply the advice, and that is the cause of much guilt, low feelings, and perhaps even depression. People are left feeling bad and somewhat unworthy of success for not having the "commitment" to their goals sufficient to make lists and break them down on paper. Indeed, this reality feeds into the experts' promotions of their books and seminars. Someone is always claiming that he or she has the right answer or approach, some way to sort out your planning and goal-setting. I am sufficiently experienced to be sure that it is not going to happen at any level close to what these salespeople promote.

Nope!

The average person (and maybe over 99 percent of us) is not wired to operate in this way. Perhaps in a military or some rigidly structured organization we might find ourselves taking that route at the planning level. Some CEOs or high-intensity sportspeople may have a higher commitment level than the rest of the population, but I believe that the best we might see is people planning their days one day at a time. This takes a lot of the planning thrill-seekers to task.

This book recognizes the many things people will not do and tries to assure readers that it is OK to be human. However, with awareness, much can be achieved. So, instead of seeing the difficulties as obstacles, readers can ask, "What can we do with what we have from where we are?"

Several questions arose during the writing of this book: How much information should I give? How much of a resource person should I be? How much hand-holding is needed? And, when the reader puts down the book, is he or she fully empowered to act, successfully, with all of his or her questions answered?

Allow me to digress a bit. Some years ago, I was on the island of Trinidad, trying to find an address. I asked a man for directions, and he started out by telling me straight up that I didn't have to ask anyone else; just go that way, then that, then...This man wanted me to have every bit of information at one time and only from him.

But my mind does not work that way. My attention span is too short to hold on to all he had to say, so I made a mental note of a significant part, and when I reached that particular place, I asked someone else. Then when I reached another significant point, I asked someone else, until I got to my goal.

This is how this book functions. Instead of trying to handle everything, it will introduce some important points and perspectives, and the reader, if truly interested in going forward in applying this information, will have to do some work to get specific answers. The specific questions will be different for everyone.

When NASA sends a spacecraft to the moon, or any faraway body, that spacecraft travels over a long distance and, in trying to get to its target, takes in much information about where it is and what it is doing, which is then fed to some compensating system to make adjustments to directions, speed, and other variables to keep it on the right track. It uses a sophisticated feedback system.

Consider the launch of a missile to strike a target two thousand miles away. The missile will go over mountains and across deserts and seas...yet a well-designed missile will have a good chance of reaching its target because it collects information constantly as it moves and compensates for the realities it meets as it heads toward the target.

It's similar in business. Goals and expectations are different for each entrepreneur, for each business, for each industry, for each era. Challenges will be encountered, and some will be better prepared than others. There can be no one set of solutions for every perceived issue that arises. But you can be sure that once there is a connection between the business operator and serious intent, and once he or she is sensitized to how things might be approached to get answers, then the pieces will fall into place. The resources and answers will become available.

The concept of critical thinking fits well here. Critical thinking assesses the meaning and significance of what is discussed and observed. Beyond logic, it gives consideration to the evidence and context, and determines the judgment to be applied. Critical thinking is vital for business success, and increasing emphasis is being placed on it in education.

The Pareto Principle is relevant, too. Named after Italian economist Vilfredo Pareto, it speaks to the general principle that a relatively few things will have a significant impact on most things and processes, as opposed to the relative many. Also called the 80/20 Principle, it suggests that 80 percent of what you achieve comes from about 20 percent of what you do. This is not meant to be "exact" in that it has to conform to a special, fixed mathematical set of numbers (80/20), but the general principle is beyond question.

In my last educational institution, we were given "resources" that listed a myriad of Web sites, charts, and other tools that pertained to the course. Most were not necessary in the sense that you were lost without them, and I ended up with a 3.97 GPA without making any attempts to "beat the system." I simply found that only a few (20 percent) resources were of major (80 percent) relevance to the course, and it made life easier.

So, as you go through this book, look at the 20 percent of ideas expressed that resonate with 80 percent of your concerns. Then spend some time to delve into those and seek the solutions to your specific situations. This is not a "hand-holding" effort, but one of creating insights.

There is a reason this book does not focus on "how to" and try to walk you through such areas as:

the business plan
the financial statements
the manufacturing
the distribution

This is because these areas comprise major topics in themselves. In addition, they are technical and thus easier to grasp or to get someone to implement.

The book does, however, discuss selling a little more. Salesmanship, perhaps, is the hardest resource to buy. The ease with which you can pull someone aside to discuss the other areas or find a model that can work is not generally encountered within the challenges of sales.

I have known business owners to genuinely believe that hired sales reps will be more committed to selling their products than they are. This misperception is subtle. After all, the owner is the boss and can hire and fire, so he or she has the upper hand. But such an expectation sets the stage for much hiring and firing unless the owner is lucky enough to hire someone who comes prepared and can drive the selling process for him or her.

There is no scientific answer for success. You can't define it. You simply have to live it and do it.

Try to make your business one of the successes, not a statistic. To be forewarned is to be forearmed.

This book is partially inspired by the book *Think and Grow Rich*, an all-time classic, by Napoleon Hill. It is about success, focusing on wealth creation, but can apply to any endeavor. Most of the details of *Think and Grow Rich* are about attitude. It describes a way of life, of looking at life, which puts the enlightened person in a mode of unusual success. Hence, it is not surprising that many successful people relate to it. Since one tends to read about these people, "success" more often than not connotes some amount of fame.

What about the rest of us? Specifically, what about the person who is curious about getting into business but is daunted by the challenges, both real and imagined? *Think and Grow Rich* might not be enough because there seems to be a gap between the principles, the motivating examples, the challenges laid down, and where you want to go.

This book will help you to deal with some of the things you had not considered before, acknowledging that their consideration now makes sense, and you will even hear yourself gasping in recognition of their relevance. It is written in plain, easy language, supportive of the theme that business ownership is about paying attention to simple things and that success is not complicated and reserved for a few chosen people. The chapters are relatively short, ending in a Small-Business Summary, for impact.

SECTION I

1. Why This Book? Who Is It For?

This book is for the small-business entrepreneur who is seeking to get started or who has been in business for a while. It is for those who want to improve the odds of success against the background of grim failure statistics. It is the product of years of research, insight, and experience on the subject of self-made millionaires and less successful businesspeople.

I agonized about the approach because I wanted the book to be perfect for those who want the right answers. I reflected on the many books I have read over the years and their collective benefit to me. I thought of the many people who have read the "classics" and have not been able to apply the information or principles successfully; some have not even made the important move to start. I thought of the wide range of people who provide business services—accountants, economists, lawyers, information managers, and general managers—and help to run other people's businesses but fail at their own. So, I decided to write on the points that are seldom taught formally. They include insights and tips addressing the subtleties that create true success.

One important point in particular will be asserted throughout the pages: success might be assisted by qualifications, but qualifications do not guarantee success. In line with this point, I decided not to write a book about, for example, planning or accounting; a business's management is assisted by adhering to accounting principles, but knowledge of accounting does not guarantee success. Similarly, identifying a particular business or industry might not help because when it comes down to the day-to-day realities, no two businesses are the same and no two operators have the same personalities and circumstances. I resisted the urge to recommend Web sites and resources because if I make the points as well as I hope, then the identification of appropriate Web-based and other resources will become second nature.

The permutations of questions and answers are infinite. Hence, my hope is to help to expand your thinking instead of zooming in on specifics that would be, for some, inapplicable and perhaps not motivating. You see, people do not refuse to get into business because of a lack of specific information. Nor do they fail because they do not know where to turn for advice and support. They frequently fail because of an unsuitable attitude toward some very simple things that are made more difficult by their approach. I cannot go further into the psychology of what takes place, but I can discuss many of the relevant points and hope they will resonate with you, bringing about "aha moments" with regularity.

This book is different and much needed in a world of "how-to" prescriptions. The reader will not be left seeking another seminar or another book or class, but will instead be left with another way of thinking. This book provides encouragement for those who are sitting on the fence. It is for the person who saw his or her friend or relative take the risks and fail. This book provides insights into what might have gone wrong or what might have been tried differently. The pages introduce important tactics and strategies for wealth creation and general success, organized in an easy-to-read format.

The book does not focus on the actual starting up of the business—the incorporation process, etc. Nor does it focus very much on the financial statements and reports. Instead, it looks at some of the attitudinal issues and other factors that are not easily addressed by neat analyses of the normal output statements.

Why one business fails and another succeeds can be an easy or difficult thing to discern. The outcome can also be truly paradoxical. A business may be run by an operator who is rude and keeps few records and reports, yet it does well. Another might be well organized and the employees very nice and effective, yet it struggles. The reason might be due, simply, to one business having the right product in the right place at the right time—great timing. The opposite, in varying degrees, might be the case for the struggling business—poor timing.

Whatever the situation, the small-business operator generally does not have the resources to withstand the vagaries of "mismanagement" for too long. Yet, everyone knows of at least one large company that is so poorly run that there is wonder at its longevity.

This book intends to help the small operator, as much as possible, to stay on a successful path. Importantly, it can help people decide whether business is for them. Many of the realities explored here are issues that might not have been considered previously. They are not optional to achieving success, and so, realistically, some people will show a sense of practicality by deciding that business is not for them. The book will have succeeded in those cases, too.

Small-Business Summary

This is not the perfect book as it cannot preempt everything and predict exactly what your experiences will be. But it can inspire the wisdom to tap into your creativity. It is about the development of an attitude necessary for success. It is for the person who wants to make the effort to be successful. Success takes more than money, more than qualifications, more than experience

2. Why Are You (Seeking to Be) in Business?

During a lunchtime chat, shortly after graduating from university, I said to a colleague, "I wish I had one hundred thousand dollars to invest in a business." He told me point-blank that I would not invest the money in a business. I was annoyed with this strong statement because he was right. I did not have any plans, any propensities, any aspiration beyond the thought that going into business would be a nice thing to do, and I continued with this feeling for years.

I had reasonably good jobs, and in my last corporate job, I felt I was building a career. It was a multinational firm, and it offered opportunities, or so I thought. Then one Sunday I got the news that my position was being made redundant. That was what drove me into business. I had little available cash, and so I welcomed partnering with others. From the challenges we faced and the speed with which people quit, I quickly learned that business was mainly about attitudes and mental toughness.

If you do not inherit a business, you will have challenges building one. So, are you ready to take on the challenge of starting a business? Consider the following pointers and questions.

Think about whether you want to work for yourself. Do you enjoy being the boss? Or do you feel more comfortable reporting to someone else?

What are your plans for the business? Do you want to sell it after a certain number of years, or do you want to work in the office only twice per week after five years? Do you want travel and enjoyment and therefore aim to get a good manager to take care of the business in your absence?

Determine how much of a risk taker you are. You must be willing to be patient and give the business enough time to get established and grow.

Consider how much time and effort go into running a small business. Many entrepreneurs have to work harder for themselves than they ever had to work for a former employer.

Find a business that suits you. Assess your skills, interests, and personal values and seek a business that is in line with these attributes.

Decide whether you want to start a business or buy an existing one. Launching a business may involve fewer start-up costs and can proceed more slowly, but the business will take time to get established. An existing business usually requires more money up front, but there might be a useful platform in place, from which one might grow quickly.

A friend of mine bought the brand and light manufacturing equipment of an established confectionary company. The brand was known and respected, and the final product price was small enough that customers gladly bought the product with pocket change. This was a very good combination, which led to rapid success. My friend, who always thought business was hard and required so much effort, was shocked by her quick progress.

Try to have enough money in the bank to get started. You'll need enough funds to pay for your everyday living expenses while sustaining the business until it turns a profit. Count on a minimum of three to six months. How closely you follow this advice depends on what is at stake (opportunity and collateral) and your propensity to take risks.

Many people will take the plunge and let the chips fall where they may. Many are very sure of what they are about and recognize nothing as obstacles; some may say they are fulfilling their life's purpose. This can be such a state of focus that it attracts the right people, opportunities, and results. These people take risks at the drop of a hat.

Join a trade or small-business association to get exposure to issues facing small businesses. However, be on guard against spending too much time on meetings and volunteering. Play your part but remember that, especially at start-up, your time will be one of your key resources.

Start to make a list of everyone you know or know about. The latter group might be people you know of but do not necessarily know personally. For instance, your cousin might work with or otherwise know someone who is good in a certain area. Your cousin constantly speaks of this individual's skills and good spirits. This is someone from whom you could get assistance, and the strength of your cousin's relationship with him or her can be very beneficial to you.

The first part of the list is easier but can be underestimated. Make a list of *everyone* you know, even including some children. Why would you include children on this list? Because children have parents who are businesspeople and managers, and your young daughter's friend might hold the key to your first order, if she can put in a good word for you, because her father buys products you will sell.

You will have to build this list over time since your memory cannot provide all contacts during one go. Simply write down all those who come to mind and cross out the repeats. Write and write. It is not likely you will ever create an exhaustive list, so, at a convenient time, start to picture how the names you have can be of some benefit to you.

And think of those names in two directions. Is there someone on the list that you can help? Is there a chance for a quid pro quo? That is, is there something you can do to add value to someone else as he or she invests some time or resources with you? This might require particular care because you can offend a person by sheepishly trying to milk him or her and offering something unworthy in return. If there is such a risk, it is better to come outright and ask for help and not simply appear like a cheapskate or some-one with poor judgment.

Back to the main issue: after giving it some thought, why do you want to be in business?

One mistake of would-be entrepreneurs is wanting to get into business to avoid the stress of large companies—the proverbial corporate world. I have heard this statement many times, and invariably, the people were do-ing poorly at entrepreneurship.

Surely, there is a particular kind of stress that comes with working for someone else, and especially with the ever-demanding work environment, it is not surprising that some want more control over their lives. But make no mistake: business is demanding for the small operator, and to the extent that this fact is not recognized, the business might stay small or die.

For example, let's say you are in business, reporting to no one, feeling a little relaxed and relieved. Work now starts at 10:00 a.m. Lunchtime is now three hours long, and it is off to the country club at 4:00 p.m. This is the recipe for failure, even if the stress has gone.

At the start, working a grand total of three or four hours per day is not a useful part of the process. Any attempt to take this approach soon results in the onset of discouragement and despondency. The business owner blames the economy. He or she blames government policies. He or she blames everyone and everything...but himself or herself. If avoiding stress means avoiding necessary work, you will fail as an entrepreneur.

The inconvenient truth for many people is that there is a price to pay. Time and effort must be invested, and there will be some periods during this investment when there is limited or no growth.

Discern the difference between what is convenient and what is necessary. At one time in the early days of my business, I thought our salespeople had to be trained since the products were technical and the economy was not exactly vibrant. We instituted training sessions that were held on some Saturdays. One of my partners, a key participant, eventually told me he could not attend because he had to take his daughter to piano lessons. That was very hard to cope with because we were both fathers of two children, yet we were trying to build a business—there was much at stake. It was not convenient for him, but it was necessary and very important to participate in these sessions. I don't think we ever made up for the decision to tilt things in favor of the piano lessons, but it was one of those experiences that will always come back for reflection. What was the correct thing to have done? To quote Stephen Pierce, the Internet marketer and multimillionaire, you cannot make money and excuses at the same time.

The truth is, the entrepreneur should be passionate about his or her venture. This causes the stress to be minimized and the time to pass without the fatigue that contributes to boredom and burnout.

But not everyone has identified that magical level of passion, so, for many, the venture simply boils down to the identification of what people need or want but find hard to get. That is the motivation behind the business, but the work required will still be significant. The process might be simple but not necessarily easy and convenient.

Small-Business Summary

Accept business for what it is and try not to attempt to work magic. Perhaps business is not for you. Many people accept this, even by mistake. Some are quite open and honest in determining that they do not want the strain of running a business. Evaluate yourself and your situation and cut your losses if necessary. Business is not to be left to chance and magic. Make decisions that are commensurate with your abilities, goals, and dreams.

3. Naming the Business

If you are about to start a small business, you are likely wondering what to name it.

Many people give in to the urge to name it after themselves. Ego can get involved, but common sense should prevail.

If you are Michael Jordan, you might wisely name your company Michael Jordan Sportswear, Inc. However, if you are an unknown George Brown, then George Brown Sportswear, Inc. might not work so well. But if you know your niche and name your firm Golf Lovers' Sportswear, Inc., then that might draw the desired customers. Or, if you are situated in a desert and name your firm The George Brown Watering Hole, Inc., then that is likely to succeed as well. So, really, it depends. How well do you know your company's niche and image, and how will your strategy fit with them?

Do not allow your ego to be the main reason for your choice of name.

Another avenue for ego-centered behavior is in the case of a partnership. If you are using both partners' names in the business name, whose name should appear first can be a source of problems. This can be resolved easily if the entity is professional, like a law or accounting firm; traditionally, the first named is the senior or more respected partner.

If the ordering of names and such considerations do not have material importance to the firm's success, decide on a strategic name, in the eyes of the prospects, and move on to the hard part of running the business. A strategic name will indicate what prospects should expect and, importantly, what will make them think of your firm more favorably than current offerings.

Small-Business Summary

In choosing a name for the business, focus on what the name means to the intended operation and how it can aid in the business's success.

4. Survival Plan

So you have decided to leave the stressful nine-to-five. Have you designed a survival plan?

Your business will grow or not depending on a lot of different factors, including the overall economic state, the location, specific market needs, hard work, and others. Your survival plan is a map toward defined objectives and time frames. This plan also considers alternatives, avoiding the need to simply react to events.

Allocate resources where they will do the best, leverage your strengths, and focus on building your foundation and important long-term objectives. Organize to track your progress with the measurement of important benchmarks that indicate how objectives are evolving against actual performance. Without a plan, you will not know what your needs are and/or whether you are moving in the right direction.

Plan for cash. Profits are not cash, and cash is not available simply because you are operating a business. You spend cash; you do not spend profits.

You have to be aware of what is going on in your personal life and with the business to make sure your survival plan is truly that—a provision for maneuvering through early uncertainties.

Current expenses must be factored in to decisions. Building your business base takes time, so ensure you have some bridging money to cover personal expenses during the early months.

Cutting expenses to the bone—lean-and-mean operating—is typically required, but everything costs money, so be prepared in the event that there are slower-than-anticipated revenues at the start.

While I do not like moonlighting, sometimes a business has to be brought to a certain level with another income in place. If the entrepreneur has, for example, a spouse providing another income, the second income provides a buffer. Without another person on whom to rely, the entrepreneur might have to remain in a formal job while working to develop the new business. If this is necessary, make sure it can be done ethically.

Small-Business Summary

Make the change to being on your own with a strong sense of reality. Resources like your time and money will be scarce. Everything requires time for building so be aware of the inevitable transition that will accompany your decision to move from employment to starting your own business.

5. Ownership/Management Structure

Most people want to own their businesses outright. In fact, many will not entertain the idea of any kind of sharing. If you can own your own business outright, then go ahead.

But you might have constraints, making it a good idea to share. Keep in mind that it might be prudent to own 10 percent of something instead of 100 percent of nothing. Also, depending on your risk profile, it might be easier to have someone to lean on for support. That said, if you have to share, pay a great deal of attention to the section on business associates later in this book.

Personally, I would avoid business partnering where there is a fifty-fifty split in ownership. I have learned that one can get into a hole of indecision and toeing the line if there is not a clear-cut person who can take the plunge and move on. On the other hand, sometimes when you have a majority owner, you may find the stronger party (in terms of shares) being the weaker decision-maker, and that creates conflict, too. Yet, as it is not a perfect world, I would not put off pursuing my dream of building a business if I were not the main party or if I could not do it alone. Many times, insisting on a particular ownership structure is an excuse for fear and uncertainty. In such a case, the person might be afraid to get into business and finds convenient reasons to avoid it.

Try to manage the ego and the urge to make it all about the personalities.

Business structure is also important. You should decide which type of business is most suitable and formalize it through registration. It can be a limited liability company, a partnership, a sole trader, etc.

This decision may seem to be of little importance now, but that may not be the case after the start-up. I believe that this is one aspect that requires a sit-down discussion with a good lawyer or accountant. Many times there are benefits to be earned by registering the business one way or the other. Also, there are pitfalls to avoid. One cannot give advice on this without specifics—type of business, location, long-term intentions, and more.

Then there is the structure within which the business operates. Try to curb the urge to have all kinds of fancy offices and titles. I have seen people invest more time and energy on the titles and the design of the business cards than on product knowledge.

Aim at being lean and mean, spending on what is essential to provide good, consistent service to your clients. All the other fluff is becoming less and less meaningful.

Small-Business Summary

Think about an ownership structure that fits your intention for the business and consider your risk profile, available resources, and long-term plan so that you optimize your interests and returns.

6. A Note on Business Associates

You may want to go into business but do not have the money or other resources to do so. One option is to pool resources by creating a partnership with someone else. This approach makes sense and can lead to success. But it can also bring problems.

Note that the word *partnership* here is used loosely to reflect not only formal incorporations into a partnership but also the simple act of getting together for business collaboration.

You might partner with someone who has a good work ethic and seems capable but never gets off the ground with his or her own business or a partnership. Why this behavior is present so often is not entirely clear to me, but there are likely to be as many perspectives as there are personality and character traits. I guess some people just need to be driven by someone who has power over them—driven by the anxieties of being hired or fired.

In partnering with someone, you might find that the person approaches tasks on the basis of what is convenient, not what is necessary. The same person who used to go to work on Saturdays now thinks that, as an entrepreneur, that is not convenient. Some of the activities required are deemed to be beneath him or her. This leads to conflicts.

Some want to focus on the pay, long before there is a capacity to pay. At the start, it is important that partners bring their seed, not their need, to the association.

You may receive many excuses for inadequate contribution. Remember, we cannot make excuses and money at the same time.

Many times, people go into business with people they know, such as friends and family. Big risk! Remember, this is your friend or relative, not some optimistic version of the person. His or her attitude will come with him or her. Does he or she respect time—schedules and deadlines? Is he or she trustworthy? Does he or she do sloppy work, threatening that the final product is going to vary with the personality of the partner who makes it?

Even though some people will never enter one, partnerships have worked in the past and will continue to work. Just be aware and be careful.

Try to balance skills and abilities. If you are the operations man, you might need a good salesman, or vice versa. Take some time to do an audit of resources, skills, and abilities. What is each passionate about and like doing? Does one party have to play the motivating role? Will everyone get into the trenches during critical times? A complementary relationship is essential.

Examine, discuss, and agree on the expectations and performance standards *before* the implementation of the business or partnership.

Decide who should do what, when, and where. Some people will accept any seemingly reasonable proposal put to them during the planning stage, especially if they do not plan to work too hard. So, if you believe that you will work harder and therefore require higher pay or special perks, work that out before the venture gets going and, in particular, before the profits start rolling in. Your underperforming partner might accept any arrangement until he sees there is real money to be made. You might wonder why someone would agree to a plan and not expect to work. This can happen because of the informal nature of some partnerships, especially among acquaintances. With the (usually) easygoing atmosphere, many people relax their efforts.

Strictly speaking, partnership agreements are drafted documents that clearly outline the relationship among the partners and their individual duties and contributions to the venture. Many possible business scenarios could arise during the partnership's tenure; they are sometimes complex, requiring legal counsel in drafting and reviewing the finished contract. If a partnership ends without a formal agreement, the guidelines of the various state laws and acts will determine how the assets and debts of the partnership are resolved and distributed.

Some issues that might come to the forefront late in the day are such things as succession, continuity, rules for buying each other out, assumed liability, etc. Or consider a less formal but perhaps no less important matter: Two people start a business from scratch. They both have customers, but one has distant customers, requiring him to spend time traveling and in hotels, getting some adventure and "perks" along the way. The traveler needs to have a bigger expense account, yet he might have less profitable customers or generate less revenue. How will that impact the other party?

There are many questions to consider. What will happen if an economic downturn comes, and the disparity in efforts and results becomes stark? What about vacation days and outside interests? The list could go on and on. The point is, you can see potential problems looming, and most times, agreements prevent disagreements.

Small-Business Summary

Knowing in advance what your needs will be helps to determine your choice of business partners and associates. Balancing your skill set with the skill sets of others is very useful, but those chosen have to be able to deliver on the expectations.

7. Considerations When Forming a Board of Directors

A small business in its infancy might not need a board of directors as much as it needs someone with whom the leader can discuss important decisions and to whom he or she listens. Someone has to challenge the leader's intentions and thoughts on the needs of the venture. Someone who is not a part of the situation has to ask questions, review decisions, and above all, push constantly to have the long-term survival needs of the new venture satisfied by building in the market focus, supplying the financial foresight, and creating a functioning management team. If the route to dealing with this important need is via a board of directors, make it (the board) small and include people who can (and will) contribute. This group must be aware of the company's strategy, situation, and prospects.

Many times the board of directors is too large or ill-composed. There are many good reasons for considering appointees to boards. Some are appointed due to shareholdings. Others might be considered because of experience and knowledge, image, or influence.

Too often, the expected contributions do not actually come from the individuals who make up a board.

No less than the large firm, the small business should have a disciplined approach to board meetings—meeting regularly and keeping proper records. The members should take their responsibilities seriously, plan, and prepare themselves to contribute.

For their part, the members should know what their obligations and possible liabilities are. It is a serious job, and it might be better to decline the nomination than to make a poor showing.

Small-Business Summary

A group of independent and objective persons can add value as a board of directors, even for a small business—but be wise enough to know if it is working out as intended. If it is not working out, you should scrap the board or under-performing members.

8. The Mental Demands of the Business

No, this is not a book about metaphysics or an attempt to demonstrate any kind of weird twists on business.

But the life of a small-business operator can be lonely, frustrating, and confusing. The required level of mental toughness is frequently underestimated, and as crises arise, the operator can buckle under the pressure of "what ifs."

Many business owners are likely to overestimate the speed some things take to occur and underestimate the resources required. As an example, suppose you need an important application document. The clerk says it takes three business days. It would be foolhardy to budget three days in your plans. Even though the firm is promising three days, you are at the whims of filing mishaps, the clerk's possible illness, or an error that requires you to come in to correct something, starting the process all over. All these possibilities and more make it imperative that you go in with a mental approach that provides a sense of reality that avoids emotional overload too easily.

The entrepreneur might see his or her inventory not moving, bills piling up, large orders canceled...the list is endless. The entrepreneur must focus on what he or she wants. He or she must think positively and avoid excessive attention to negative news, people, and outlooks that will affect him or her more emotionally than practically.

I suspect that many people will not grasp the full impact of this mental process, but it can mean the difference between success and failure—and even deep depression.

Practice good mind management. Examine what you say to yourself, your daily thoughts, and your feelings. For example, if you believe, as some people do, that money is the root of all evil, then will you truly extend yourself to earn, manage, and defend profits? Are you inclined to cut your prices every time someone whines about them? Do you have a strong sense of and commitment to a reasonable and desired markup for your goods and services? Do you believe that business is the right and privilege of a chosen few? It will be difficult to operate for a long time if you are out of sync with your core beliefs and values. Many people struggle with such issues and wonder why a near-perfect business idea did not succeed.

Consider this. Some MBAs, professional accountants, economists, and other professionals who are well trained in areas of business are unable to start or run a small business successfully. It is not because of a lack of knowledge. There is a side to business that is beyond business.

Success goes beyond qualifications and experience; in the entrepreneurial sense, it is a result of setting goals, focusing on them, and applying determination and courage. These attributes are not taught easily, but because of their importance, it is not surprising that people endowed with these qualities succeed without a high level of formal academic training.

Success starts and ends in the mind. You should consider why you expect people to come to you. You do not have a track record people can use to search you out, so you have to become an expert at some profession or master an art. This requires strong will and determination, and these are driven by a strong desire to succeed.

Strong desires automatically set priorities and discipline. Discipline is not something required as an end in itself. The desire brings forth the discipline. This is why Tiger Woods spends hours hitting golf balls—he needs to be able to master that art so well that the golf balls go where he wants them to go. A sprinter has to practice hours a day at fast-paced running. A yogi has to practice sitting in meditation for hours per day to develop spiritual focus. They all have to invest the necessary time. So to be called "disciplined" means you are developing your skills. It takes time.

The need to invest time was strongly emphasized in a presentation by Stephen Pierce. He said that people oftentimes do not factor *time* in to their expectations. He illustrated his point by stating that a couple would not expect to speed up the period for pregnancy simply because they want to have the baby in three months. Having it in three months presents a problem. Some things require a significant and purposeful investment of time, and where those things create value for customers, the businessman should have the discipline to invest time in the process.

In essence, the businessman must have a clear vision that will inspire discipline and purposeful work, leading to the creation of value for the client.

Motivating yourself will be an important aspect of your daily routine.

Picture this. You get up for work one morning, and your whole family has come down with the flu. You have ten deadlines to meet that day, and the price of one of your key input commodities moved up by 25 percent overnight. It snowed a foot last night, and the car won't start. These are but some of the scenarios you might face.

The successful process starts with your commitment to a clear purpose.

Can you depend on you?

Normally we consider whether we can depend on someone else, but very often it is we who let ourselves down. What are your needs, your fears, your strengths, and your weaknesses?

Consciously map out a system for your education and development, incorporating motivational videos, CDs, role models, coaches, experts, and anyone else who can be there as an example to call upon for support in your weaker areas.

Most times, you will be your own coach, mentor, and cheerleader. Therefore, you must first believe and, second, follow through. In the midst of it, remember that we are all driven by our emotions. The mystery of man is that between our physical bodies and our emotional selves, we can become confused and lost. Some emotion is making you do certain things, take certain actions, and feel a certain way, and the sad part is that generally we do not understand ourselves. We want to succeed but do not understand the reason we are feeling the way we do—we just feel that way. And we respond in ways that make us feel good, whole, nourished, or sad—any reaction that feels right.

It is therefore not surprising that we have a fear of failure. Perhaps more surprising is our fear of success. Our fears are driven by the way we perceive our world, and so we might believe that we do not deserve certain things and sabotage ourselves with denial. We all consciously want success, but subconsciously, we can do and attract things that make that success unlikely.

We can focus on the need to eat a certain way, to do some chores, and to see our friends and relatives, but then not do these things. We are held back by our emotions. We are held back by some power stronger than our conscious selves, and yet it is clearly we who can change our habits, our wills, and the course of our lives.

Our emotions get in our way and rule our actions. Consider the habit of smoking. By now we know better, but we still focus on being happy for the moment. Similarly, the need to make one more call or spend one more hour at a task or write one more sales letter is stymied by the urge to party or join friends at the club, and this is the reason why only a few make it to the top of excellence.

Only a few are driven by an ardent desire, iron will, and alert intelligence. The latter makes them set strong priorities and less likely to miss opportunities.

To operate successfully in business under difficulty, one must first learn what mental qualities are essential and how to gain them. But there needs to be balance and caution. For instance, in the quest, try to avoid the perfection trap, which is procrastination in disguise.

In the past, I have had tasks to be done or challenges that simply required a start and took on the philosophy of "one more..." Thus, my approach was to see if I had one more book on the subject or one more seminar or one more opinion. I found that making a start is, in many cases, a lot more meaningful than additional information. Once you start and commit resources, you gain more purpose to your activities.

Sometimes external factors help to propel things forward. Hence, having paid for an application or rented an office or ordered some stocks, you automatically have to do more things to move toward your goal.

As you deliberate the issues, you will decide whether to go forward. Again, my mentor Stephen Pierce sums it up well. He said that you might have decided to do something while making a reference to the future and how good it would make you feel if it worked out—how you would enjoy the outcome. That reference had a positive impact. Or you might have decided not to do something, thinking about the past and how you knew someone who tried and failed or was embarrassed about some aspect of the outcome. That reference had a negative impact.

These are the scenarios that make your qualifications, cash, and experience not very helpful in your venture. So become aware of what is happening—how you think, how you feel, and how you respond. Awareness is the first step to self-mastery.

Small-Business Summary

Your mental state and approach will contribute most toward your success. How you perceive the world and its challenges will determine how you respond to the day-to-day developments and opportunities. Beyond business management, proactive mind management is the key to success. Optimism, determination, focus, and other positive mental attitudes will be necessary to reach your goals.

SECTION II

9. Pay Attention to Systems and Structure

The small-business owner can have a nagging feeling...What happens if I am not available?

Some see this as a good thing because it means they are indispensable. Others would identify it as a threat and be concerned about continuity.

If the entrepreneur intends to sell the business, he or she will want to communicate some sense of continuity and have systems in place for handing it over.

But even if the entrepreneur has no plans to sell, there should be a sense of order. He or she should aim to have the business run smoothly without him or her. After all, why leave the formal job to slave for the business?

Hence, he or she should document systems and processes. Evidence of the need for this type of documentation shows itself in everything being referred to you. See if any of this applies to you: You are in meetings, and people call you "urgently" to find out who the contact is at this or that supplier. Or, they are blending a product and have to vary an ingredient, and you have to be contacted to remind them how much to use or how long it should take because no one else can do the calculations, etc. Something happened in the business two years ago, and you are called to remember how it was handled. There is a piece of software for doing routine work, and when it comes to handling certain bits of work, you have to be the one to organize access or to do that difficult little part. Customers need discounts and explanations, and you have to be called to work it out and/or approve them.

These are just some of the things that can happen day after day. Once you take a hard look at the situation, you can organize to make it work better and require less of your personal time and energy. Thus, the small-business operator should document contacts, suppliers, ideas, challenges, assumptions, quirks of the business, customers, customers' special needs, etc. Once documented, the information is available to staff who can access it without referring to the manager.

See yourself as so organized that you can go off and relax. Alternatively, use this organization to impress the people you want to buy into your firm. Leverage technology and get the business working for you, not the other way around.

Planning to have things going on without you might be the best plan.

Most people have an aversion to precision, it seems. Sometimes when I mention some simple ideas, people look at me as if I am giving them irrelevant work. For example, I use a Palm Tungsten, which is backed up on my PC, and recommend that others use similar strategies. Every time I come across a business card with some relevance, I enter the information in the Palm—at least I try to most times. I also try to link the information so I can search for some detail I might forget later and not sure where it is to be found.

For example, if I am at a seminar and meet someone who is able to give me information on a novel piece of equipment that will stand out, I will place some reference to the equipment in the person's general information area. That way, if I am struggling with the name, I can enter the equipment, and when the general information comes up, I scroll around to find the contact information I need.

This works very well in other areas, too. If I hear about a new restaurant or hotel I want to try, I make a note about the interesting food, the location, or the entertainment; years later, I have been able to find such information, even after changing my PDA.

I do not like detailed work, and fiddling with gadgets does not inspire me too much. That has kept me using a few Palms because I find the information transfer easier when they crash or otherwise malfunction. I do not try to keep up with the latest because, as with cell phones, computers, and software, I use a small fraction of the power and hype.

When I got a BlackBerry, I tried to upload the information from the Palm into the phone, and the fields did not always merge very well. Sometimes when I search or receive an identified call, there is a mismatch of information. Therefore, my Palm is invaluable, and using the full features of the phone is a chore. I am relating all of this to recommend that each small-business operator have an easy (preferably electronic) way to store and retrieve information.

As for the point of planning, you not only need to have access to the information, you also need to plan to have the system and the access. People are always asking me about names and numbers, etc., simply because I make an effort to store them in a simple and organized way. While I cannot claim perfection, my system is extremely useful and time-saving.

So, here is what the small operator can do. Make a list of all things to be done in the business on a day-to-day basis and the other tasks for different periods. Involve others, and brainstorm to find the information and processes that could be organized better.

Ask yourself if you can put your hands on files and information relevant to the issues. What about important contacts and processes? How are some decisions made? Are some decisions too much within your sole control? What changes can be made, and who else can be empowered to share the burden?

Years ago, we had a simple formula for a blend of a product borne out of experimentation. It was not in high demand, and I was involved in most of the initial preparation and sales. I am ashamed to say that, even years later, when the subject came up, people always had a tendency to call me to verify or approve something regarding the product. This wasted a lot of time and placed more demand and stress on me.

I should have made sure that everyone involved in the matter understood the issues and their roles. Then we should have recorded information and explanations, which would have avoided my later involvement every step of the way. The added benefit here is that such an approach makes it easier to achieve the continuity mentioned before and adds value to the business.

People are always impressed when they see that there is evidence of thought and organization in a business's operations.

Small-Business Summary

The small-business owner can go off in quiet moments and assess how well the business is working for him or her and whether he or she is working too much for the business. Especially if manpower and skills are scarce, he or she should think about efficiencies to be gained by implementing sound systems, and how he or she can reap the rewards of entrepreneurship faster and in a more fulfilling manner if he or she can work himself or herself out of the business enough to enjoy the fruits of his or her labor.

10. What Business Are You In?

What business you are in does not have an absolute answer, since similar enterprises can successfully define their businesses in different ways.

A shopping mall, for example, can define its business as a real estate business and drive its efforts on the basis of maximizing returns per square foot. Another might define its business as the entertainment business and drive its efforts on the basis of providing people with many options in entertainment and food.

If you own a pizza shop, you might seek to be in the "lunch" business so patrons know they can stop in during lunchtime for good, fast pizza. Or, you might be in the "evening meal" business, offering customers many options of snacks and dinners.

It is necessary to discern what business you are in.

By defining (or redefining) your business, you can apply creativity and open up a new way of viewing the business. Additionally, this helps create a niche that gets you to zoom in on customer needs and how to serve select groupings efficiently.

Sometimes you find that some types of customers are simply a headache to deal with. They do not seem to fit in with your profile, resource base, and what you want the business to do for you. By defining your business appropriately, you will cut down on the number of such customers. Our company had a customer who used to buy an item that was sold in a case of twelve. This customer used to ask for six cans only. We would sell those six cans to him, then keep the remaining six cans for a long time, until someone else wanted six cans. This seemed like good customer service, but in reality, it was more costly to do it this way, without any commensurate benefit to the firm. This "flexibility" was in fact a distraction.

You can define the business to address more lucrative or otherwise more profitable niches.

There is a story about how the old-time railroads thought they were in the "railroad" business and did not adjust to competitive pressure and changing times. It is thought that had they defined their business as "transportation," they would have been better able to respond to market changes and needs.

It is from this perspective that you are encouraged to deliberate this point and see how best to position your business—in search of a lucrative niche.

Small-Business Summary

Understanding what business you are in also helps you to uncover what business you ought to be in, in order to take advantage of developments and innovations in the marketplace and in entrepreneurship.

11. Product Selection / Market Selection

Really, the issue is all about your niche. Is your product in demand? Can demand be created for it? Does your business provide experience or expertise within your niche? Is the organization a learning one? Can it adapt and make changes in approach as realities are uncovered?

It is not uncommon for entrepreneurs to leave their original places of employment and set up businesses that respond to niches their former employers refuse or are unable to serve. Some enter business with an idea and soon recognize that they cannot succeed within the framework of their prior understanding.

Usually small businesses are built around some experience the operators have. For instance, they may know the product, based on some prior hands-on experience. They then decide to go into business applying what they know, and it works well.

But there can be challenges, too. For example, a mechanic leaves his job to open his own shop. He seeks to take the customers he used to serve on behalf of his previous employer. He may not do very well because warranty issues keep customers away; warranties are sometimes voided if owners do not use approved repairers. Also, he might be good with the spanner and screwdriver but a poor business coordinator. Instead of being a direct competitor to his former business, he might do better to seek an alliance, if possible. His business might be a good avenue through which his former employer can outsource work.

Another example of a sector that encourages employees to venture out is stationery supplies. Stationery suppliers and other businesses that are relatively simple and allow employees to develop strong personal relationships with customers might entice the employees to venture out, relying on the relationships to generate business. But, very likely, the entrepreneur lacks the economies of scale and the designing and printing finesse. His or her contacts, formed when he or she was in a big firm, might not lower their standards.

In selecting a product, guard against friendly advice without substance. This is a good recommendation.

For example, you tell your friend you are pursuing this or that venture, and he flippantly advises that there is no market for the service, even though he cannot back up this statement with any kind of research. Conversely, some well-meaning individual hears someone ask for a product in desperation and determines that there must be a significant market for it.

Try to see your choice to its logical conclusion. Beyond the start-up, is this the right product or market or framework that is going to work for you?

Small-Business Summary

Your choices of products and markets are significant and cannot change overnight. Be sure to have the right products and markets well defined so that they are in sync with your resources, capabilities, and efforts.

12. Selecting (or Reviewing) Your Niche

I know someone who considers diverting the course of her business every time she sees evidence of someone buying a container-load of a particular product and "making money from it." Fortunately, so far, she has talked about these ideas more than she has acted upon them.

Can that approach work? I don't know for certain, but I suspect, strongly, that the odds are against it.

The small-business operator should have a niche to ensure efficiency and effectiveness.

It might be a niche in terms of customers, or a niche in terms of products, or a niche in terms of geography, or a mix of all three.

With the usual scarcity of resources, one cannot hop around hoping to take advantage of every perceived opportunity.

More than one business is seeking opportunities. Skill sets and experiences are different for each of us, and even finding a cheaper source of some product or raw material does not automatically create viable opportunities. Business, especially a modern one, requires focus—a focus of intent, a focus of resources, and a focus of thought and energy.

Buying a container-load of an item and making money is at best a project. The life of it might not extend beyond the current container unless the person can see a spin to the situation and, with experience and qualifications, truly build on it for the long haul. If an entrepreneur suddenly finds something unusual and there is a market—like an easy way to heaven—he or she can make money for a time, but he or she should look out for the herd of competitors coming his or her way.

The entrepreneur must be diligent in identifying and selecting a niche and find a way to provide value to that preferred segment.

When the time comes, the entrepreneur has to be ready to narrow his or her focus and deal intelligently with the marketplace.

In the past, suppliers of goods and services were good at cornering the market—hence, the idea of the one-stop shop. But it is almost impossible to pay attention to all aspects of a large, modern marketplace, so smart people decide to focus on smaller and rewarding parts. Oftentimes the big firms that operated by spreading themselves too thin did not know what was happening in their industry until it was too late.

So, decide on your niche.

Is there a way to look for those customers and prospects in a certain area? Should you decide based on socioeconomic grouping? What about the prospects' profiles? (Even in a simply defined business, such as being a self-employed accountant, some prepare themselves to work only with small businesses, as opposed to large ones.) Be alert to what is happening and how people are currently complaining, relocating, or making adjustments in their affairs, and you might find niches that are opening up or not being well served. And so on...

Select a niche that you know about and that involves something you care about. This is vital because you will easily spend the required time on a subject if it is more than just a business. I've noticed that many auto parts merchants are strongly into motor car racing. That is an area of passion for the enthusiasts, and they attract like-minded people.

Aim to become an authority so you can validate your interest and command attention and respect, leading to charging a premium for your goods and services. It is the way consultants and specialists operate.

In taking your strong passion, interest, and information further, you can back up your approach with a Web site and e-commerce. This really opens up a world of opportunities because you can write and sell material, instruct and teach, and grow your business in many ways, even transcending your national borders.

Small-Business Summary

Carefully seeking out a niche and serving it can be a most efficient and rewarding approach for the small-business owner to consider. This is an area of preparation where you can do much thinking and brainstorming, drawing on your mentors and coaches—the opportunities are truly endless. It is not easy to tell you how to find your niche without some sense of what you do or what your interests and core skills are. However, once you apply the general principles of strong observation and the will to learn, you will uncover a niche. One note of caution: if you are starting small and do not have some sense of delimiting your market to apply focus, you are likely to be heading for trouble.

Consider this: The very successful former CEO of General Electric (GE) led this huge corporation, made up of many companies and divisions, with a view that said if GE was not number one or two in the particular business, then they would not remain in the business.

13. Building from the Base

Good record-keeping is essential for any organized activity. It is of great importance for business. It can be very disconcerting to see a small-business person with a wad of assorted documents that date back months or years, hoping to reconstruct some record for the auditor, banker, or other interested party.

But things do not have to be like that, and sometimes all it takes is for someone to introduce a simple computer-related system—even a simple Excel file can be an effective start.

From a simple system, one can take action. Looking at your customer list and knowing what products you sell, ask yourself some basic questions about their buying patterns and behaviors and act on the answers.

Specifically, the use of a record-keeping system can help to avoid what I call the "ninety percent syndrome." This is when one loosely says things like, "Ninety percent of our customers buy this or that." Or, "Ninety percent of our customers are located here or there." Aiming to have reliable information and to make decisions based on fact and reasonable assumptions is the mark of management integrity. It is amazing how one's assumptions can become unreasonable because they are skewed by likes and dislikes—perceptions based on small or rare incidents that took up a disproportionate amount of attention, etc. This is one reason databases have so much versatility; they can be configured to give good information.

What prospects fitting the desired profile can be converted into new customers? This question might seem simple, but do not allow the simplicity to hide the importance. Many times it is because we can relate to the success of a previous experience that we have the confidence to act on a current opportunity. Hence, a prospect with circumstances similar to those of a current customer is a candidate for your services. The key is to avoid answering the questions superficially and to act on the answers.

Your business sells to a certain type of restaurant. From your records, you can see that others of a similar type might be converted because they have common problems or needs.

Considering your current customers, what more can you sell them? Again, this might seem simple, but once you have the customer already enjoying your services and experiencing a good relationship, you can ride the connection.

Usually, it is more difficult to sell to a new customer than to a current one.

But it sometimes requires the intent to satisfy more needs or wants. Consciously deliberating the question makes one see natural links among interrelated products. For example, a customer buys tires from an auto parts business and buys gas from your gas station. The customer sees your stock of tires and yet continues to split his purchases. One day, someone asks him why he doesn't buy tires at the gas station, and he shrugs and says, "Oh, sure!" Sometimes it is as simple as that, but it requires some intent to make the move.

Keep your current customers happy. Think about it. Most interactions in life eventually get taken for granted. I cannot help smiling inwardly when I am in a forum where sales reps refer to buyers as "my customers." Two weeks or two months or two years later, you might hear that the customer has stopped buying. The same sales rep now insists that the prices have gone too high or the company "ran out" of the product, and the customer switched.

Let me tell you, it is hard to discuss such developments with a defensive sales rep. He or she will find a million reasons to explain why the customer left, as long as it is not attributable to him or her. But, most often, it is the apathy with which the customer had been treated that created the opportunity in the first place. The tradition of dropping off a token at Christmastime is not going to stop a customer from moving on.

Customer relations have been the subject of many texts. A few business owners have spotted niches arising out of customer service gaps in the marketplace that make such niches viable, but even those creative people soon start to miss the ball.

The focus required for customer service and attention that builds long-lasting relationships that protect business is uncommon. The ability to sustain such focus would make one's reputation legendary. It is the root of keeping the customer truly happy. It can be done. Everyone prefers to buy from a known and trusted source.

Find organized and ethical ways to keep your customers from leaving.

Small-Business Summary

At any point in time, your current customer list is your base. Build it, keep it current, and treat your customers with the care that shows them that they are the key to your organization's success.

14. You Don't Have to Reinvent the Wheel

The progress of business is the reason for millions of meetings being held every day. Many are for the purpose of finding out what changes can be made to get better performance. Typically, the question is: what do we need to do differently? That is, what new product should we seek, what new location, what new sources, what new customers...?

Those questions all have merit. But I have a feeling, based on my own experience, that we should invest more time in exploring how to do what we do now better. This does not necessarily mean applying better technology, but applying better discipline. This simple observation can make a difference.

Remember your niche? What will happen if you jump from one "opportunity" to the next outside of your niche? Soon, you send mixed and confusing signals to the market and to your stakeholders, including employees.

Let us suppose that a current, small customer was buying ten dollars' worth of our product per week, and we managed to move them to twenty dollars' worth per week. Shouldn't that infer something about what we can achieve by paying attention to the customer who buys one thousand dollars' worth per week? We can double our business with a few large and medium-sized customers and dramatically change the profile of our turnover and profits!

Yet, we may spend most of our time debating how to get another Chinese manufacturer to send us a container-load of items of uncertain demand, suitability, and turnover.

Don't get me wrong; expansion can come from various approaches, and there is nothing fundamentally wrong in seeking new products and sources. Sometimes that is what is required.

The point is that we usually have a significant opportunity to build on the base, and as someone observed, if you cannot bake one cake properly, it is pointless asking you to bake ten. Too often, the drive to expand stems from the business's underperformance—not that the business has exhausted its potential in one mode but that there is the perception that it will do better if it gets into more areas and more products, offers more discounts, etc.

At the least, use your current situation as a guide for performing well.

Small-Business Summary

Sometimes useful change comes from improvements in what we do now, not necessarily in seeking to do new things. Underperformance can be a sign that we should improve our skills and capabilities, perhaps leading to greater opportunities later.

15. Insights into the Business Planning Process

Worry does not help, but if you must...worry before it is time to worry and develop a contingency plan.

The business plan is not something that most people look forward to creating. Indeed, perhaps many people who look forward to the plan are those least likely to implement it. I compare business plans to résumés. There are an almost infinite number of options and ways to approach the writing of such documents, and many people devote much time to "getting it right."

I Googled "business planning guide" and got 269 million hits! It is mind-boggling to think that there are 269 million genuinely different perspectives on preparing a business plan. I think the diversity stems from the various nuances people bring to the process. Some planners emphasize the financials; some emphasize market research; some emphasize the SWOT (strengths, weaknesses, opportunities, and threats) analysis; some focus on developing strategies; some agonize over the differences between tactics and strategies; some focus on the "now," while others focus on the "future"; some highlight the production aspect, while some focus on the human resource needs...and the list can go on.

It is almost heresy not to have some sort of a written business plan. This document helps you to see what issues might be concerns or create opportunities at the start. It is your road map.

This is in spite of the fact that a written plan is seldom consulted later. The more elaborate the plan, the less chance of it being used, it seems.

The reason for this is that oftentimes the plan is a project. "We will take the last week in September for a planning retreat," says the head office mandate. The retreat usually has nice food and accommodations, perhaps a well-known motivational speaker, and much numbers-crunching with the best PowerPoint presentations. But it does not usually deliver useful results.

Later, the business gets in the way of the plan.

I can recall encountering the nicely bound report of plans two or three years later while going through some long-forgotten drawer. (Interestingly, I remember smiling mischievously over an old group picture and wondering how so-and-so had gotten so fat, being less concerned about the benefits derived from the planning session.)

The small-business person seldom has the luxury of being able to arrange retreats. Yet there is merit in some kind of a plan and its execution for the small business.

Americans, some say, had an advantage along their path to global domination. With two great wars leaving their infrastructure largely unaffected and the economic benefits as suppliers and experimenters fully exploited, they did not need long-term plans.

Or did they?

Indeed, there are many tales of large businesses starting from the jottings on a small napkin over lunch. Yet, the Japanese, it is said, plan for up to 150 years ahead. So, is it a cultural thing, or is it a planning thing? Or somewhere in between?

While it is good to have a plan, the marketplace is not aware of it and usually has a few surprises in store. So the plan's assumptions can become irrelevant quickly.

Still, it is good to start with a plan. It helps to cement intent and examine assumptions, and provides a framework for deploying your resources. Because it is so much a game, it requires feedback from the environment because, like most games, one does not know ahead of time what moves the opponent will make.

So it is with the small business. You have to look for the openings—your niche. You move into the position that offers the most options and assess the chance of success or failure, depending on what moves the opponents make and the viability of the customers or niche. Then provide the best service you can, while keeping your eyes on the competitors.

Al Ries and Jack Trout introduced the concept of bottom-up marketing, referring to the idea of seeing what is happening with the customers at the tactical level and using it to redefine the strategy.

Consider a posh restaurant situated near the Twin Towers in New York in September 2001. It might have been doing great providing businesspeople with fancy lunches, based on an upscale plan. Come September

11, business stopped for the high-profile customers, but the hardworking people doing recovery work needed fast lunches and refreshments. Such a restaurant then might change its direction overnight and provide lower-scale meals.

Such a practical move—with a change reflecting the reality of the marketplace and ignoring the initial plan—could save the business.

The small-business owner must have the discipline to start and finish a plan. Yet, he or she must have the flexibility for adjustments – as we have seen.

I am examining this topic from several angles because so much comes down to intent, as well as discipline and attitude. An interesting thing I have noticed is that in a class of business students who have a business plan to produce as a project, some students will get an A for the project but go into the real world unable to create a practical, implementable plan for a business. A few students will seek to use their firms as the subject of the business plan and might add some value to their firms if they share the information, while another set, a very small minority, will develop and implement a plan to start a business they have dreamed about. These are the minority for two possible reasons: either they are very diligent, or they have hit their passion and it propels them toward success.

Some people spot an opportunity and design a brief strategy around an idea. It might be the supply of a product using low prices as the strategy, or fast delivery, or some form of valuable convenience. If you spot a niche, it is usually easier to develop a plan around the perceived unique selling proposition (USP). Using that to branch out into a general plan works because the person tends to be focused and energized toward something that he or she is passionate about.

But, in general, there is something funny going on with respect to creating and following business plans. Getting some insights into this fact should help the business owner to be aware of the challenges and the pitfalls. In my opinion, it is not enough to make a big deal about planning, knowing fully well that the process or the output will give people nightmares.

While I do not claim to know the reasons behind the attitude toward plans, I am fully aware of the effect of this attitude toward them. Having made the point that planning is important, I would not be satisfied to simply leave the reluctant client in a quandary. So, what I try to do is come from several angles with the premise that it is OK to have a particular view or approach to the subject and not be rattled into inertia. This is my main point. Even if you do not like planning, you can succeed. You do not have to get it "right"; simply get it going. Perfection is the fertilizer of procrastination because it provides a good excuse.

If you like planning, you can still fail. But by approaching your situation calmly, you can get assistance and run your business successfully.

It is not easy, or perhaps not as productive as it might appear at first, to write a useful book on business planning. Because of the challenge that businesses face, many books seek an optimum solution. But because each business is different and because authors usually place emphasis on their own pet peeves, the ideas and approaches might be skewed toward personal circumstances or challenges that weigh down the reader. But the process can be less burdensome if the person knows that it is OK to have left out some things in the first year, or the first draft. There is no easier way than to follow Nike and "Just Do It!"

One article said that a sound business plan is your road map to success. What characterizes a sound plan might provide another 269 million hits but leaves the apprehensive person with more questions about his or her readiness to make the first move. I would not even suggest a particular Web site or an approach beyond encouraging synchronicity between the business's needs and resources. I doubt any one expert can claim to be the end point of information for all businesses.

Some of the questions that will help you find the right resources regarding business planning are:

What are your main priorities? How can you allocate resources where they will do the most good to your interests?

Do you want to guide your firm to growth, or do you, for example, want to manage your cash better? Is cash flow tight, and does it require special considerations? Do you have enough cash, and when might you need some?

Who should be responsible for certain priorities as you identify them?

How will you track the progress of your aims and priorities?

What are your strengths and weaknesses in relation to, say, production or marketing?

Answering these questions makes it somewhat easier to get going and to develop a more substantial plan over time (the proverbial bite-size approach), if planning seems onerous and frustrating. Remember, most small businesses fall short here, and it is not particularly useful to chide them or to get the managers to read another book and get another spin on the reasons. The focus should be on how to make people comfortable with their planning process and to provide practical help to get them moving.

Consider a person who has a simple business—he sells newspapers to people driving by an intersection, going up to cars and offering his product. Deciding he wants to be a good businessman, he comes up with a simple plan. He devises a way to remember all of his customers' names then addresses them by name. He offers a lollipop to their children and always has a bright smile and words of encouragement. Soon, everyone looks forward to buying from him—indeed, to greeting him each day.

His approach seems like a good plan for him, and he should have a lot of goodwill soon. The approach is simple and what is required by the business. In a more complex business, the owner might also use similar degrees of simplicity, knowing that big results invariably come from a combination of small but important actions. So the owner zooms in on the priorities and implements them.

The bite-size approach can work, and as the business grows, the owner can purposefully employ someone with the experience, training, or temperament to undertake this important task. In addition, the employed person will have fewer reasons to avoid creating the plan (because it is delegated) than the owner, who can agonize over it but is not sufficiently driven to act.

This point might seem odd, but it is the oddity of human behavior. Some individuals will work a lot harder for an employer than at their own businesses—in spite of the claim that they want to be their own boss. It is because of oddities like these that writers have difficulty getting the perfect approach to the plan.

My guidance is this: Do not try to find the perfect business plan template. Choose one and work with it. Additionally, do not try to incorporate everything in your small-business plan. If you try to do this, there is a big chance of being overwhelmed with the implementation and you will likely not attempt to do most of what you've included. You might also experience some dissonance or emotional discomfort with the disconnection between what you think you are getting done and what your plan says you should be doing.

This point is interesting. As stated previously, there is something that takes place in the mind that gets us to sabotage our plans or intentions.

If you are uncomfortable with how you approach your projects, you will procrastinate, and the mind will provide very good reasons for why you are not making progress.

I have a friend who discovered a business prospect. He prayed about it and felt so strongly it was what he wanted to do, and an interesting thing happened. He started to get anxious about the business plan, especially the financial aspects to do with the costing and other areas. This was someone who had an MBA and worked in a field that required him to do costing as a major aspect of his marketing job. He developed insomnia and other symptoms of anxiety, such as jitters. Then one day a good friend and partial mentor suggested he work with a particular accountant, and together they developed a plan and ran some numbers that projected very good revenue and profit. The night after they finished the outline of the plan, his sleep was the best he'd had in weeks.

Like most challenges, business is a mind game, and emphasis on some aspects of it will be very negative for some.

Be warned. It is foolhardy to start without intent, commitment, and some form of a plan, including some ways to test if you are on the right track. Having said that, do not get bogged down with the plan itself. If you have to second-guess the details, and if you have any feeling of inadequacy or discomfort, it is a sign that there is dissonance. Evidence of this might reduce your commitment to the plan or the planning process. If that occurs, seek advice and get started on the business. Any little success will be motivating, and as time moves quickly, you will soon get the point of not worrying because the plan was not perfect.

Small-Business Summary

Do not take any of this to mean a plan is not necessary, just that it is OK to have jitters, or uncertainty, or failures, or to recognize you need to improve upon it. Just stay in the game and get help, preferably bite-size help that addresses specific concerns and not an overall analysis of whether you can or cannot write or implement a business plan. In the long run, it will be your diligence—paying attention to the little things that make up the big picture—that will be most significant to your success.

16. Promotional Awareness for the Small Business

I saw a brochure produced by an insurance company. The front had a lovely picture of a couple, supposedly showing the joys of owning property. The second page listed some reasons to choose that company for your insurance needs—knowledgeable staff, corporate stability, financial strength, claims settlement (i.e., claims are settled promptly), competitive rates, great products, and other claims.

The third page listed a set of questions about the company and new services. The fourth page itemized the things one has to provide when insuring a new vehicle. The list seemed long ("You will be asked to do this and that...")—all sounding onerous to me.

The fifth page listed vision and mission statements, accompanied by the company background. The sixth and final page listed all of their offices and contact information.

I have done business with this company for a few years. They call us mainly when it is time to renew, and the reason I read the brochure was because I had to wait more than the promised five minutes for my receipt after making a payment.

Would I inquire about their services now? Not really. I already know them.

No one bothered to ask me about any other needs I might have.

My point is that this approach will not serve the small business that has to find and excite clients. I am not convinced that many will respond to the inward thinking that informed this brochure.

Apathy is one of the poisons that kill a small business, or any business for that matter.

Indifference is what usually evolves from a business (in fact, any) relationship that is taken for granted. This again is where Internet marketers have responded well because they do not have an option. The customer can only be reached via some form of constant communication. Good Internet marketers are always searching for ways to make a new offer, such as an offer of something of value that is free, hardly allowing you to forget about them.

The ironic challenge for a business is that oftentimes the firm recognizes the threat of apathy and tries to keep in touch with the customer. But the contact at the customer location will frequently respond by saying he has no time, everything is fine, he will call you, etc. Chances are he will not find the time to call, even if he has a problem. Sometimes he does not realize he has a problem. You wait, and some astute competitor's sales rep visits and takes your business.

The next time you visit, the customer will tell you many things—he was not able to contact your firm, he has not seen anyone for a while, he was able to get a lower price, etc. This is an emotional response to the fact that you are, after all, business associates and he feels bad about having given the business to another person.

Find ways to keep your presence with the customers even while you are physically absent.

Give your clients a reason to want to do business with you. Do not assume that they know what you do and, in spite of the current relationship, that they will call you when opportunities arise. Oftentimes, they don't even know what is an opportunity for you!

Out of sight is out of mind.

Some people utilize loyal account programs. Perhaps the most popular example of this is airline frequent flyer miles. The airline might provide crappy service, but the free miles are worth the hassle. If you get "a better price," you will have to wait to build miles with the new company. Be careful, though, about ethical considerations. Some laws and states might not be in concert with loyal account programs or might tolerate only limited aspects.

A small business can offer discounts on purchases above certain levels or on purchases over a certain period of time. Another thing it can do is offer related products free of charge. For example, let's say the firm services photocopiers. It can offer a free toner every six months if it does a certain amount of servicing. This provides the customer with an incentive to call.

Deals should be open, fair, and kept within legal boundaries and company policy.

Going back to the insurance company cited above: For the brochure to promote the firm, people have to read it. Of the few who read it, fewer are likely to act on anything stated therein.

The small business can hardly afford to invest in materials with such a small chance of success.

Small-Business Summary

The small business is better off appealing to customers' hearts. Hence, relationship selling is key. Since they are less likely to have big brands, small businesses have to strive to be first in the minds of customers when it comes to certain types of solutions. They must make sure they are providing true value that can be defended. Many decisions are made from the heart and defended with logic. For example, when a maintenance supervisor buys from you because you are a nice guy, he has to defend this decision to the finance VP by pointing out that this was the fastest service he could get or some other such reason.

17. Customer Lists

Let us again consider the customer list that was introduced in chapter 13. This is perhaps the most important list that you have. It includes qualified customers who know and understand how your firm functions. They know you are nice people, and they do not have to wonder if you will deliver.

Most new prospects are not as comfortable with you. Yet they have a need for things you sell. Whom should you focus on?

The easiest person to sell to is the one who knows, understands, and trusts you.

Working diligently with your customer list can lead to many, many opportunities. Once you have an up-to-date list and understand the customer profiles, you can get to work.

Working closely with the customers on your list can help you find out several things. For example:

- Who can buy larger quantities—the up-sell
- Who can buy related items—the cross-sell
- Who has outgrown their current model and can get better efficiencies (or would be happier) with a newer one—the upgrade

Let's say your firm sells vacuum cleaners. Your customer inquires about model 30, and you qualify him for two because you find out he has two locations. This is the up-sell.

Figuring your customer needs mops and brooms in addition to the vacuum cleaners, you sell him yours. That is the cross-sell.

He buys and is happy. But later you inform him that there is a new, more expensive, bigger vacuum that can save him energy. He buys it. That is an upgrade.

Consciously thinking about your business and your customers can improve the value of each customer significantly.

A simple example of the cross-sell occurs at a church. After collecting the tithe, the preacher offers a collection of books, CDs, and DVDs. Selling these along with the sermon is considered the cross-sell.

But how do you get customers to buy in the first place?

Let's face it. There are many people offering their products and services, and just as many are claiming to be the "best." The key is to consider your niche and find a way to make an offer that simply cannot be ignored.

Narrow your focus and find that irresistible unique selling proposition (USP).

The ubiquitous money-back guarantee has lost its impact by now. Even though there is some reassurance that you can get your money back, sometimes the process is designed to frustrate. Yet, it was revolutionary when first introduced.

One USP that created quite an impact on consumers, and is examined in many business books, is the move by Domino's Pizza to guarantee delivery within thirty minutes or it is free. Some people might not be impressed with the pizza's taste, but many like to put Domino's to the test.

Thus, the challenge for many small businesses is how to stand out in the crowd.

One can only act on specific information. What are the market needs? What are the competitors doing (planning)?

In all of this, understanding your processes and your costs is the key.

Things can be challenging, but you need to move to excite your prospects into action, and you need to do it within a framework of acceptable or desired profitability.

Consider two basic approaches. One is called a single-step approach, and the other, a multiple-step approach. You can make a single-step promotional move by placing an ad in a magazine or newspaper—anywhere that a prospect might see it—that calls for some action. The prospect might call in to request additional information, for example. But the probability of this evolving into an order is low.

You can take a multiple-step approach in seeking to get a more qualified group of people to respond in such a way that you can intensify your focus on the promotion and improve your chances of conversion. In this regard, an e-mail list can be useful if you can get it. E-mailing (or normal mailing) to a group that has demonstrated a prior interest (or interest in a related area) takes you closer to a more direct relationship that can be beneficial.

Let's assume you are selling a health-care product, like a range of organic foods. You can place an ad in a widely circulated regional publication and offer interested people a free report on the dangers of pesticides and the health benefits of eating food grown with natural fertilizers. Ask interested readers to send an e-mail and request their free report.

Many people will not be interested in organic foods, or they will not make any special efforts to get it, like spending more for it. Such people are likely to ignore the request.

Some people will be curious, and some will be very interested. They are the ones who will ask for the free report. In asking for the free report, they provide their e-mail address, and you can now speak to them about things in which they have demonstrated an interest. The cost of promoting to this group will be lower and the conversion rate a lot higher.

So that brings us back to understanding your costs. You can offer other things for free if you know what they cost you, their value to the clients, and how much they might affect your overall business.

As time goes by, you make more generous offers and you give your prospects reasons not to opt out of your list. There will be related ways to expand the list and modify it as the business evolves. In the meantime, you are up-selling, cross-selling, and applying network strategies to earn greater revenue from your base of original customers.

Small-Business Summary

After deciding on your niche, you can get an even better focus by finding a way to be in touch with people who not only fit into the niche but demonstrate an interest in the products or services you provide. Direct mailing and the Internet provide good ways to communicate with such people, letting them know what you are offering and giving them good reasons to buy.

18. Creating Opportunities Using Free Offers

Research whether you can provide services for free that other providers charge for.

Remember, the small business has to be creative and make opportunities.

Some years ago, at the start of a chemical and lubricants distributorship, we would accept almost any proposal that would give us a presence with a customer. We did lubricant training free of charge—at the customers' locations.

Businesses that offered this service typically invited a large number of workers from various customers' companies and either charged for it or used it as a PR event. We went directly to the customers and saved them time and money. Additionally, by imparting knowledge to a set of interested customer employees, we made them more open to hearing about and discussing our main products. We had a captured audience.

One can do audits, surveys, training, cleaning, etc. free of charge. This provides good field experience, networking opportunities, and goodwill.

Here is an example from *Guerilla Marketing Weekly Intelligence:*

Case in point: When an apartment building went up, signs proudly proclaimed that you get "Free Auto Grooming" when you sign a lease. Soon, the occupancy rate was 100 percent. The salary they paid the guy who washed the tenants' cars once a week was easily covered by the difference between 100 percent occupancy and 71 percent occupancy, the usual occupancy rate in that neighborhood.

Your task is clear: Think of what might attract prospects and make customers happy. Be creative. Be generous. Then, be prepared for a reputation embracing generosity, customer service, and sincere caring.

Today's customers are attracted to giver companies and repelled by taker companies. What kind of company is yours?

Also, make yourself available on weekends and public holidays. Many clients and prospects who work on weekends or during late shifts are not very busy—there are no phones ringing, and most of their coworkers are off. This provides the ideal opportunity to hear of the real problems and the solutions they are seeking. Your commitment to do this builds rapport, relationships, and business in a significant way.

Even a talk with a low-level technician can provide the insights to do your homework, get a sense of the company's headaches, and make a powerful presentation to senior management at a later date.

How?

By getting the full scoop, you will have information superior to your competitors'. So, while they focus on the price and the discounts, you zoom in on the meat of the matter: the customers' headaches.

Do some things for free and reap the rewards later.

Small-Business Summary

Doing some things for free can appeal to the human instinct for minimizing risks in decision-making, and to be sure, if your service betters the competition's, you are likely to be rewarded with paid business later.

19. The Importance of Good Preparation

In these turbulent times, how can you compete, truly compete, effectively? Good preparation is essential for effective competition, and it starts with doing your homework.

As a student, I developed the habit of paying attention to my homework, almost passionately. This was because I noticed, very early on, that those who did their homework got better grades, in general. (I was not fooled by the few who had the knack of beating the system.)

Homework is important to business, too.

The minute I hear about a product that poses a challenge or an opportunity, I check up on its supplier, the customer, the price, its acceptance, its faults, and where I think it is going. I do my homework.

Many times your representative will tell you he or she has been displaced because of a better price on the competitor's product. Very often, some homework can provide the facts that tend to find your team member napping. That is, the loss has more to do with inadequate attention to and preparation for the customers' businesses.

I recall one case when a competitor was selling a spray grease that competed against ours. Our cost was about 40 percent more, but their can stated it went up to 450 degrees Fahrenheit whereas ours went up to 500 degrees. This difference was perhaps insignificant for practical purposes, but it saved the day when the customer was encouraged to buy a little room for comfort.

Gather competitor and customer information. Understand it. Understand what you can do with it.

In most fair negotiations, superior information leads to more favorable results.

Small-Business Summary

Your business is influenced by the customers, prospects, and competitors. The more you know about all of them, the better your decisions will be.

20. The Importance of Strong Customer Relationships

Have you ever had a truly nice customer who buys a lot and likes you, but the relationship is really driven by only one contact there? What happens if that contact leaves?

One has to wonder how a customer can buy a line of products for years from a good supplier, but when the customer contact leaves, all of a sudden the new decision-maker has lost confidence in the line.

I have known a customer to buy $100,000 worth of products, and simply because of a personnel change, that stopped overnight.

When you attempt to get to the reason for the customer leaving, you get many different explanations. Sometimes it comes down to the fact that the present incumbent has "his people." Sometimes sales rep apathy causes him or her to take the business for granted, and during a visit three months later, after the suppliers realize that nothing is happening, he or she provides some lame excuse. Whatever the explanation, the small business must understand this potential threat and plan for it.

The small business has some built-in disadvantages. Oftentimes its brands are unknown or its resources too small to provide massive promotions and backup service. If the firm is distributing XEROX brand copy paper, it is luckier because some large firms will insist on the branded paper. If it has a generic brand, it has to make some special efforts at getting or maintaining a presence.

One strategy to adopt is to understand the dynamics of the client's operation. If it is the job of the client's office manager to decide who gets the orders, find a way to get introduced to his or her boss and build a relationship.

Try to let the boss know how much you have been saving his or her company and how much value you have been adding to the business.

In this way, if the office manager leaves, the boss has an incentive to continue with you.

If the firm is large and has several departments, systematically find the key contacts in these departments as a strategic way to network within the account. That way, if a department is closed, you have other income streams there. Similarly, if a department head is changed, you can call upon the others to vouch for you.

Research some vital area of your client's business or industry and give them a free report. If the CEO sees how much interest you take, and especially if the information is instrumental in saving them time or money, he or she will be grateful.

But this effort has to be made long before the change; otherwise, it will seem corny or disingenuous. You need to do this while relationships are strong.

Small-Business Summary

Understanding your customers and adding value to their businesses provide a sure foundation to build a successful business relationship with them.

21. Understanding Your Competitors

Some time ago, the company I worked for had a significant piece of business with a customer, and we felt secure in having a logistical advantage over our main competitor. However, we woke up one morning and the business had gone to the main competitor. The new general manager appointed by the competitor's owners was living in the same gated community as the customer's general manager. What would have happened had we known these two were neighbors?

We should seek to understand our competition. The above example is not unusual. And the advantage does not have to be so dramatic.

Make it your duty to know and understand your top competitors as well as you are expected to know the customers.

The customers are in the business of making money themselves, and none of them is immune from that offer they cannot refuse.

Know your competitors: talk to them; study their products; know what their customers think about them and their services; know how they approach their business. All of this can help to identify opportunities for you or help to avoid surprises.

As another example, a customer who grew to be very pleased with our service depended on us in many ways. They had previously bought a product from a large competitor, which was stocked under the competitor's brand name. Our office was confused when the customer faxed us a request to supply it. I knew what the product was and uncovered our equivalent. Deliberations involved technical considerations, so we had to know what was what. The customer bought our product at a higher price than the competitor's, was happy with the performance, and continued to use ours.

If you are operating in a small community, people will call asking about products. Knowing what is happening in your industry can create opportunities. Very often the customer just needs a solution and does not care who provides it.

So, knowing what is going on can lead to sales opportunities.

Small-Business Summary

If you understand your competitors' interests and how they operate, oftentimes you can find ways to "undercut" them apart from cutting prices.

SECTION III

22. The Selling Process

Do not be fooled by the brevity of this chapter. The selling process to bring in revenue is the most important in the business. That is why much is discussed in later chapters about sales reps' behavior and their selection.

In a small business, everyone is a sales representative.

At the start, a small business can be a one-man band. Sometimes things evolve into the establishment of a firm with a large, dedicated sales force. But whatever the size, the process starts with the answering of the telephone and is influenced by the way commitments are handled.

Does your firm follow up on promises? Many of us talk about the proverbial intent of "under-promising and over-delivering." It is usually more talk than action but is sometimes achieved.

But the sale does not end with the delivery. The product must be correct and suitable for the application, and the after-sales service, including the investment of efforts to understand the customer further, will lead to building on the base as time goes by.

The selling process—planning, promoting, offering, closing, delivering, and dealing with debtors—is a chain of activities around which the firm is organized. Sometimes it is handled by one person, and sometimes many. It requires excellence in all areas.

Small-Business Summary

Conventional wisdom had that a sale is not complete until the customer pays. Nowadays, that can be modified to "until the customer makes a repeat purchase." Such is the current nature of competition that the firm has to organize, not for after-sale service, but for repeat sales.

23. Reviewing Your Pricing

Small businesses sometimes get their pricing wrong.

Businesses might go too low or too high on pricing because they either do not factor in all the inputs or do not factor in the market forces. Indeed, they might even go too low because they do not have a sense of what margins they need to make.

As an example, an operator buys a product for ten dollars and marks it up by 50 percent, or five dollars. He sells it for fifteen dollars and does not recognize his margin is only 33 percent. He knows his markup is 50 percent (maybe he even sees this as high) and considers his margin to be the same percentage. This simple example is not farfetched, and the operator who makes the error is not stupid.

Symbolically, the margins tell you not quite how much you make in terms of how much you added but how much (and this is the key) you keep after paying for costs associated with making the product, as a fraction of the sale. Many times you will get a sense of what the impact of your pricing is by talking about the percentage margin you make. This also allows for a comparison with other businesses or industries. The fuel retail industry tends to have a standard margin (or ranges); the construction industry will have one, as will the airline industry, etc. When you compare the actual margins being made, you can get a sense of a firm's specific performance in this area. (This is of particular importance if you are seeking to assess a company's stock value or attractiveness.)

If you have to pay commissions, delivery charges, and other such obligations, understanding this becomes even more critical as you might find you are retaining very little to cover overheads. In the example above, when the business sells the product for fifteen dollars, it makes a margin of 33 percent (the five dollars) for overheads and profit. So the operator must have a sense of what this means for his objective of trying to make sufficient margins to cover expenses and to make a net profit.

Markup versus margin: The margin emanates from the markup. The markup percentage is higher than the margin percentage, but their dollar values are the same figures. In one sense, the margin tests the markup for adequacy. If the businessman marks up by 100 percent, the margin is 50 percent. So, 50 percent of what is collected is held back for expenses and profit. If the markup is 200 percent, the margin becomes about 67 percent. In moving from a 100 percent to 200 percent markup, the margin moves by only about 17 percent! If you mark up by 300 percent, the margin moves to 75 percent.

In the latter case, if a product costs $100 to make and is sold for $400, or at a 300 percent markup, the margin amount and the markup amount total $300. If the administrative expenses are high—in particular the marketing and selling costs—the margins can be eroded without your realizing it. Hence, if a sales rep earns 25 percent commission as a fraction of the selling price, that means that $100, or a third of the markup amount, goes for that purpose only! What about other marketing expenses?

That is why the actual dollar values become relevant. On high volumes of production/sales, the aggregate revenue more easily meets the overall expenses, after direct expenses like commissions are taken out. So, in our example, where the markup is 300 percent, the gross margin per unit is $300. The rep gets $100 in commission, leaving $200. If the overheads are $200,000 for the period, then the firm must sell 1,000 units to meet them. You can see that as the sales volumes go up from 1,000 units, more and more revenue is generated to leave enough, after expenses, to meet the overheads and make a profit. Lowering overheads also makes the objective easier to achieve.

A friend was in a small manufacturing business and was reportedly doing OK. He did not seem to be concerned about the number of customers, but I noticed he kept running out of cash. He took a few bridging loans and was not paying himself a salary. His product price was achieved via a meticulous pricing process, and much of the business was COD or very short-term credit.

So why was cash so tight for this firm? The possibilities were:

1. The receivables were not being collected.
2. There was some draining of funds from the business, not recognized by the operator.

3. The planned margin was not adequate.
4. The actual margin was not in sync with the plan (if, for example, the firm was discounting and not making up with volumes to compensate for net lower margins, this can happen; or, production costs were rising and not being reflected in the prices).
5. The sales volumes were too low.
6. Expenses were higher than projected.
7. Some combination of the above points occurred.

The business made attempts mainly to find extra cash, not to uncover the reasons for the shortfalls, and the business got further and further into trouble.

The above example emphasizes the point that the small-business operator must have a constant sense of the suitability of the margin, the competitive arena, the base costs of his or her goods and services, and the operational expenses.

Previously, I made the point that you ought not be bogged down by the financial statements at the start. They are best understood with practice and advice. As the business unfolds, you can make the connections and combine the theoretical with the practical. Some business students have difficulty with the connections, however, and that is why I discourage attempts to get it perfect before you get going.

Eventually you will have to become familiar with this area if you are going to operate effectively. Chapter 36 examines the main financial statements, and jumping ahead a bit, the profit and loss statement, figure 1, shows sales of $370,000. The cost of goods sold is $70,000. The gross margin is $300,000, or about 81 percent. The markup is about 428 percent. As high as it seems, it might not be sufficient in some cases, depending on other factors, especially expenses.

Therefore, one value of this financial statement is to provide a reality check. If your intention in setting the selling price was to achieve a margin of, say, 90 percent, that is not being achieved in reality. This is verified by the information contained in the income statement, and so the statement is the performance benchmark.

After setting the selling price, a monitoring of the income statement can test what is being achieved over a reasonable period. Reasons for variances can be discounting or rising costs that are not being reflected in higher prices.

What about the psychological aspects of pricing?

Pricing does not always have to do with how much a product costs; perhaps, more important, it is how much people think it is worth. I have been in situations where the prospect was so impressed with what the product did, I could have picked a price from the air and still walked away with a sale.

If you examine past and present sales, pricing policy can be assessed. For the faster-moving products, you can increase prices, and for slower-moving products, you can decrease prices. This can have the effect of improving revenue and perhaps reducing or increasing demand, if either is desirable.

If you are unsure about this important aspect of your business, seek advice. Many people will not be able to grasp the mathematical nuances very quickly. This is fine. Just seek someone who is experienced in business, costing, or accounting and ask him or her to explain and show you the details with examples.

Paying someone to walk you through or critique your pricing can be a very, very good investment.

Small-Business Summary

Setting the correct prices for your goods and services is important to your survival. It is important to check your inputs and assumptions from time to time to make sure there are no surprises lurking in the shadows of your calculations.

24. Be Wary of Discounting

Many people will ask for a discount, and some will insist on it. Some businesses will be railroaded into giving one.

Typically, people who ask for a discount are looking for about a 10 percent reduction, and often, the seller agrees to it.

If you mark up a $100 product by 100 percent (not many of us can do that) and give a discount of 10 percent (i.e., $20) off the selling price, you actually lose 20 percent of the markup. Your effective margin has moved from 50 percent to about 44 percent (remember, this fall allows you to keep less money for contributions to your overheads), and the dollar value of your net revenue (after costs) earned has moved from $100 to $80. At the full price, the margin percentage is 100/200, or 50 percent. With the discount, the margin is 80/180, or 44 percent. You need to consider the above scenario and be confident about the wisdom of the discount, or at least how to figure your discount policy.

Most salespeople do not consider this computation and that, furthermore, there is commission and perhaps delivery and other costs to add in. Your overall margins might turn out to be too small, being a fraction of what you originally planned on. Many times we focus on the increased number of sales we get or expect to get, but things do not always work out favorably. Depending on the campaign, you can end up simply discounting to people who would have bought at the higher price anyway.

How does discounting fit in with the wider strategy, and can the general turnover afford it?

There is a chain of restaurants that sells on the basis of "all you can eat" for one price. I know of a smaller restaurant that promotes "all you can eat Thursdays." I often wonder how the latter decided on their strategy. How many more people eat on Thursdays who would not have otherwise gone to the restaurant, and perhaps more importantly, how many people who would have had their meals at full price on Wednesdays or Fridays go and get their fill on Thursdays instead?

I also know of a haberdashery that offers 10 percent discounts on Wednesdays. However, when I go there, I do not see them trying to make add-on sales or any other moves that seem geared toward optimizing the revenue from people who come out to take advantage of the discount. I therefore wonder what the reasoning behind the strategy is. My wife simply goes on Wednesdays to get her items. How does that work out for the operators?

The trick, I am sure, is to understand your costs and be familiar with your target market.

Many small businesses are spooked by customers insisting on discounts, and sometimes the reality is that discounting cannot be avoided. However, do not be caught off guard, and make sure that underlings have the appropriate authority (and understanding) to offer discounts. Hapless discounting can cause your revenue to leak away from your business. Discounting goes straight to your bottom-line—lower profits!

One thing the business can do is seek a quid pro quo. If the customer insists on a discount, then seek a larger purchase of the same item or an add-on of another item.

Keep in mind that you can flatly refuse the discount. Sometimes the customer is only testing, and it is his or her right to request a discount.

Note that when the roles are reversed, you should ask for discounts as well.

Negotiate everything…

Small-Business Summary

Have a sound policy on discounts and make sure everyone understands the implications of giving or not giving them. Be sure to know how the lost revenue will be made up.

25. Alternatives to Selling for Cash

This is a big problem: there are times when your products simply do not move or movement is inadequate.

The small business seldom has the flexibility of the big, established business. There is usually less credit available, and expenses like wages and salaries have to be addressed in a timely manner. Apart from commissions, wages and salaries are coming around in spite of whether or not you sell your products. If you need cash, you have to get creative at times.

What should the small operator do?

If the problem is not a lack of financing but the inability to sell the product, then the movement of the product must be the main focus. If the product is right for the market and the times and sales are still slow, then promotions and advertising are what one should look at first. Let people know what you have and how it can work for them. Then offer incentives for them to buy. Give them reasons to act now and explore the options of suitable packaging, distribution, credit, and discounting that can help to get people buying. Sometimes during a cash crisis, profitability becomes secondary.

What about bartering? Search Google for "modern bartering" to get some ideas pertinent to your business. According to the *Colorado Springs Journal* in 2004, bartering accounted for over two billion dollars in goods traded among North American companies. Bartering is a business idea. Money is a way to measure value, but it does not have to be exchanged directly for every transaction. Someone has something of value, and you have something of value. Relating these things to money sets a benchmark of value, and you can exchange knowing that there is some agreement of fairness.

Centuries ago, traders did just that. It was normal to offer, for example, cotton in return for tea and other such commodities. Moving along the trade route, the astute trader knew what was needed where and what was available.

Look at what you sell and who might need it. Then see what these people might have to offer. The deal does not have to involve the exchange of money.

What about reverse buying? This idea has fewer possibilities but is still something to look out for when your hands are tied.

Years ago, we sold a product to a firm, and they had stocks that were not needed because the equipment was not in use anymore. We were able to buy back the remainder of the product at a much-reduced price and sell it to a similar manufacturing firm at near market rate. This was a win-win-win for all concerned. Opportunities like this come from a good understanding of your business and customers—and having a good relationship with them.

Buy items on consignment. Many items can be obtained on consignment, meaning that the seller understands that any stock in good condition that is not sold will be returned. This is used by people who are planning a party and are not sure how much liquor will be consumed. The day after the party, there is a tally and a return of unused items, and everyone is happy.

Cash moves both ways. It goes out when you spend and comes in when you sell. Hence, when you have stocks of anything that you do not need, they have tied up your cash. So, if you are unsure about how some items might move—whether in your production process or otherwise—you might convince a supplier to get into an arrangement like consignment. If for some reason the seller is more optimistic than you are about the prospect of selling the items, then he or she might quickly agree to such an arrangement with you.

Small-Business Summary

If your product is not moving, you have to examine several options. Test to see if the product is right for the market, if the price is right for its value, if there is need, or if there needs to be promotional initiatives. If you need cash fast and there is no financing available, you have to become creative and examine such things as bartering and reverse buying. Your cash flow statement or cash budget is a key document to determine when you are likely to have cash flow hiccups. It can help you to spot the needs and make suitable plans before the situation turns into a crisis.

26. Maintaining Market Focus

The small-business operator can start out as or evolve to be a hustler, mainly because he or she is usually more informal in his or her decision-making and can do things more quickly. The expectation of being nimble or flexible can divert attention from his or her main focus and create confusion in the minds of everyone, including the customer.

As stated before, the business owner needs a niche. In today's competitive world, everyone needs to understand what business they are in.

I know someone who started a business within a niche—selling agricultural chemicals and fertilizers. He soon branched out into all types of chemicals, including household bleach. He even went to household devices. He sought to satisfy every demand he heard about.

The original market was changing rapidly, and he could not cope. Soon the other items got in the way, and eventually, he was not able to support the building he bought. It was just a matter of time before the bank stepped in and took over his assets.

The real problem is that many people see what they think is an opportunity once there is "great demand" for any item. Critically, this shifting to a different product diverts resources, and the firm has to reorganize to communicate to and serve this new market. During this time, what is happening with the old market? How long is the learning curve for the new market or product?

If something is worth doing, it is worth doing well.

Here is where things get dicey. Let's say that a firm is doing OK selling pool maintenance products. The operator comes across a good source of paints at a good price. He figures that as he is visiting homes to maintain pools, he might as well offer painting services, too. He invests in that aspect of the business, and the original people in the paint business drop their prices.

The pool customers know that the pool maintenance suppliers are good guys, but business is business and they should have competitive prices. In order to compete, the pool maintenance people are forced to shift resources to see if they can win in the painting business. Whatever the outcome there, the pool maintenance aspect of their business suffers.

Consider another small business selling maintenance chemicals. There is no middleman, and they make a high margin that allows them to pay a reasonable commission to sales reps, who are selling directly to end users. Someone suggests they sell consumer items to such customers as gas stations.

Gas stations seek to sell fast-moving items (i.e., inexpensive) and want to get as much credit as possible. The maintenance chemicals business has to pay transporters to get the goods out. They do not have a relationship with the supplier (their source) of the consumer items, so they have to prepay for the goods and also pay up front for the customs duties, etc.

Hence, they get distracted trying to source an elusive cheap product and in the process minimize their operational margins. They consider making some investment in promotion and also offer the customary discounts and credit to the trade. Once things get going, resources are needed to keep them going. What happens to the original business?

Have these changes ever been done successfully? No doubt they have been.

Should you do it? Think carefully about that.

This is not to say that a business should not seek opportunities. Rather, it should assess and understand whether there is indeed an opportunity and learn to say no.

Small-Business Summary

The temptation to go after every seemingly attractive opportunity must be resisted if the business is to avoid spreading its resources too thin. Unless the business understands the market and is able to demonstrate a clear competitive advantage, the operators ought not to think that the indication of a few sales necessarily constitutes a true opportunity for diversification.

27. Assessing Your Success

You will have to assess your success periodically. Different businesses will emphasize different measurements of success because of how convenient it is to do so in a relatively simple way. Even nonprofit organizations need to have measurements to assess their performance. Let's examine key performance indicators (KPIs).

A key performance indicator is a particular indicator or measurement of an organization's performance in some area of its operation. It is a general concept, with different emphases depending on the type of business and goals of the firm.

One type of KPI might be financial ratios that can help to determine how effectively and efficiently a business is operating. This information is usually best benchmarked against a similar business, similar in size or industry, to make sense of it.

For example, the return on assets (how efficiently the firm uses its mainly non-human assets) of a small business might be much higher than that of a big business without any regard for practical efficiency. But the most common KPIs are the measurement and reporting of sales, profits, and costs. These measurements are what are most likely to be found in a small company. If you get into larger or more complex businesses or industries, you might encounter KPIs like sales per square foot or dollar sales per employee.

The business owner should sit with his or her accountant or an experienced businessperson and discuss, based on the nature and stage of the business, what KPI might be useful at the time. He or she should determine how to get about three periods for comparison. For example, in looking at sales for the second quarter of the year, he or she can set side by side:

Sales in Qtr 2	Sales in Qtr 1 (the prior qtr)	Sales last year (Qtr 2)

In this way, he or she can see how well the business has just done, how it did the period before, and how it did during the same period last year. Important bits of information can evolve.

For example, if the business is selling greeting cards, months with dates including Mother's Day, Christmas, Father's Day, and so on will be expected to generate more business. The business operator should not expect October's business to be as high as December's. Without much insight into the greeting card business, I would guess that one expects October's sales to be at about the same level as August's—unless the business is new and one expects growth month to month as the name gets established. If October's sales are higher than or close to December's, there is a need for some critical thinking about the business; it might suggest that the business is declining in some way. Other possible reasons for December's sales to be lower than October's are equipment breakdowns, industrial action (strikes), raw material supply problems, problems with large customers not ordering, disasters causing transport and delivery hitches, etc.

These numbers about the business will impact you differently, depending on your role or your location. Many of the observations mentioned would not be surprises to the management. Yet a shareholder reading the information online might see some news that will affect how he or she views the investment—is it properly managed? So you can see that information will have relevance when comparisons are made and when explanations are given.

One key success benchmark is the actual plan or intention from the start.

What did you set out to accomplish?

In this regard, a fourth set of numbers would be needed for the example given above. What were the budgeted sales for the period?

Fundamental targets on sales, profits, number of customers, margins, bad debt, costs, expenses, etc. can be planned and assessed periodically. Year-to-year comparisons are vital to check how business realities are changing and how the business is learning and adapting as time goes by.

You cannot manage effectively what is not measured. A tracking system is driven by documented plans and procedures backed up by collection and analyses. Information must be relevant, have regular frequency, be current, and be specific so that there is no ambiguity when the stakeholder reads it. These requirements make it important for the small business to implement software to capture and manipulate data—such an approach will be most efficient.

Small-Business Summary

A hair salon may notice that the bulk of its revenue comes from repeat customers of the same hairstylist. This type of business requires repeat customers, and they are aggressively seeking to improve here. KPIs show that as customers get more comfortable, they spend more. Hence, the parlor wants to move more of their business toward repeat customers and the steadier, long-term cash flow they represent. One of the most important KPIs for this company is therefore the number of repeat customers a hairstylist gets. By tracking which customers request a hairstylist by name and have been in before, they are able to accurately calculate this KPI. They may then set a specific goal for their KPIs, such as 50 percent of customers being repeat business, and track how their employees meet this KPI. Employees who meet or exceed the target are rewarded, while employees who fall short are given further training in order to achieve the KPI target.

28. Learn from Failure...and also from Success

Many times we glibly talk about learning from failures. By failure, we mean that something has not worked out quite as well as we intended. When things go as expected, however, we pat ourselves on the back and live happily ever after.

I have had many salespeople open their eyes wide in disbelief when I asked why they were successful in making a particular sale. Most want to simply take all the credit and wonder why such a question would be posed to them.

But the question is simple and deliberate. If you want to expand, you should seek to expand successes. If an operator in the fast-food industry were delighted to find a product that released the operator to sell more hamburgers, wouldn't another such business be happy to hear about it?

Ask yourself, "What problem did we solve, and who else has such problems?"

A corollary to this is to ask for referrals. People in similar industries know people in their neck of the woods with similar headaches. The referral is very qualified, meaning that this referred person needs your product and will be motivated to act upon hearing that his or her colleague is happy with your product. This will make him or her want to purchase the product a high percentage of times.

In fact, it is a good habit to ask yourself "why" constantly. Then follow up with "how can we..."

This empowering question can open up the creative process.

Small-Business Summary

At some stage, you have to accept that certain actions will not bring the desired results and move on with the lessons from those "failures." However, also observe keenly what things are working, inside and outside of your firm, and duplicate those things that make a good fit.

29. Perfection vs. High Standards

You should try to set high standards for the service you provide. You need to have high-quality employees. However, you should not aim for perfection.

Perfection has an alter ego: procrastination.

Many times people with good ideas sit on them, awaiting that perfect time, that perfect product, that perfect person to come along—or that perfect plan.

Perfection is an illusion.

A high-performance team can excel at tasks when its members take their roles seriously. There is an inexplicable energy that one feels as a member of a small team working with purpose. Success breeds success, the saying goes. When you are working out a problem and everyone is in sync with the objectives, the ideas flow and the answers come; time seems not to matter. No one worries about the missing apostrophe or the misspelling. Indeed, mistakes happen less frequently because people, generally, are more motivated toward achievement, and the little things get done better, resulting in better big things.

The suitability of staff plays an important role. A qualified, motivated, and empowered employee fits into the picture more easily. Remember, the caution against a perfection drive is not to suggest tolerance of incompetence. But many times the reason for low standards stems from the poor choice of team members. In such cases, when output standards are raised, the capability mismatch creates stress, and what might be a normal expectation based on the required outputs (for competent staff) manifests itself as a drive for perfection (by substandard staff).

Another reason for the perfection quest is the fear of failure. If the idea of failing puts you into mental convulsions, then you might send out stress signals and become a perfection seeker. This places unrealistic demands on both you and your associates. This is especially so if team members are not qualified or otherwise able to measure up.

Some signs that might indicate the perfection trap are:

1. Not forgetting errors.
2. Hating to lose and never letting go.
3. Not recognizing a middle ground (always all or nothing).
4. Hardly seeking help; you know it all, and you do it all.
5. Being overly persistent. (While persistence is good, spending your energy on too many small things can only be draining.)
6. Constantly finding faults.
7. Being driven crazy by cluttered spaces and resenting those who operate in this way.

Small-Business Summary

Make your moves. While you should not set out to compromise with substandard work, do not delay a move because there is just one more thing to make it perfect. You don't have to get it perfect; just get it going.

30. Dealing with Debtors

Being forced to sell on credit can be a drain on some businesses. Lucky is the person who can get good credit terms and sell for COD or prepayment.

The situation is worsened when other components of the sale have to be settled before you get paid. For instance, a tax component may become due for payment and paid long before the customer actually pays.

We have an independent contractor who delivers goods for us and is very reliable. However, we sell to the customer to whom he delivers at net thirty days, and he brings in his invoice for payment a day or so after the delivery. He is adamant about his payments being made quickly, so instead of arguing with him, we have used him less and less over time.

If a business finds itself on the edge, it must consider some options. It can seek to change selling terms if the customers are agreeable or if the market situation allows. Note, however, that some customers might switch to a more lenient supplier.

Sometimes the simple truth is that the business needs to be more efficient, deliberate, or purposeful in its receivables collections activities.

A friend of mine went into business and was excited about the prospects. Everything seemed to be going well, and the business did not have a high day-to-day cash requirement. After about a month of vigorous selling, it suddenly dawned on him that he had been ignoring the receivables that were accounting for over 50 percent of sales thus far. Such a thing can happen easily.

In spite of your best efforts, some customers can be difficult. One way to protect yourself is to make sure that all paperwork is done and all the customers' needs are met. For example, some customers want particular documents to go to different departments and locations for different reasons. Some customers need multiple signed documents and will not pay on, say, a faxed or photocopied document. The seller must understand the nuances and organize to work with them. You could find that after having given thirty days' credit and the time has passed, you then start to chase the payment and suddenly realize that processes of investigation are now introduced, setting back payment for another thirty days.

Another type of difficulty arises when the customer has all the documentation but is a habitual bad payer out of spite or has serious cash flow challenges. If your goods and services are essential to his or her operation, you can demand prepayment, post-dated checks, COD, or any method that can shift the balance of power in your favor. Remember, once you have passed on the goods, you have lost some of, if not all, your leverage.

One tactic is to get a commitment from a suitable department head, the manager of the firm, or the financial head. Tell him or her that you will supply the goods if he or she can make a promise to pay at the right time. This clearly is not foolproof, but it provides a subtle avenue to be able to call the official and remind him or her of the promise...yes, some people do feel obliged to act on that. A stronger approach (for example, seeking prepayment) might cause the competition to be invited in.

Receivables management is important for any type or size of business.

Here is the key: the sale (and profit!) is already reflected on the profit and loss statement, and the manager can look good even if the overview is too superficial. There will be "profits" being made without any cash flowing in. The business might be starved of cash and might even be borrowing to maintain its position.

Cash is king and must be free to rule; it is not to be kept tied up in receivables.

Let everyone know the importance of collecting and devise processes to ensure success.

Small-Business Summary

The money owed to you, especially if it emanates from your expenditure, via manufacturing, for example, is a significant source of risk to your business. Indeed, the sales leading to these receivables contribute to "profits," and you have to pay taxes on them in many cases. This area must be well managed as it can lead to downfall, even in a booming economy.

31. Dealing with Creditors

At the start of my business career, I visited a small-business owner and witnessed him reluctantly take a call from a creditor. His secretary did not screen the call, and so he had no choice but to talk.

He was on the phone for some time, making promises and coaxing the person on the other end of the line. After about fifteen minutes, the conversation ended, and he was mad at his secretary for passing on a call from someone to whom he owed money.

I was amazed at this. I was sure he was not in such a mood when he first received the goods or service.

He later had to close that business, and the last time I saw him, he was bouncing around, trying to get another one up and running.

I believe one of the things that can help a small business tremendously is to take a positive and responsible attitude toward creditors and the payment obligations to them.

It is a sign of integrity to respect people who provide you with their services.

Also, I believe that the time and emotions spent in dodging creditors is totally wasted. That time can be spent seeking ways to improve your operation, and the credibility gained from a responsible approach can help you later.

For example, the minute you have doubts about your ability to pay, call the creditor. Nothing helps more to disarm a hostile creditor, unless, of course, you are calling with the payment. Talk honestly. Be up-front about the difficulties and offer a credible promise or payment schedule. Most times, it will be accepted and save your reputation.

Next, pass this attitude on to your staff, and organize your business with a view to have your debtors pay you as well as you pay your creditors. The advice of "do unto others as you would have them do unto you" is very applicable to this matter and will be a life-saver.

When things are particularly bad, seek a moratorium; see if some of the debt can be eliminated. Offer some shares or an interest payment. See if there is a way that the debt could be canceled, for example, by way of an exchange in services. Any serious exploration of options will show serious intent and will help to protect your reputation and integrity.

Taking the view that for your business to succeed another should suffer is really no way to build a foundation.

Small-Business Summary

If you do not take your obligation to pay with the same seriousness as you do with getting paid, you have a significant gap in your general management that will affect your reputation and, ultimately, your ability to do business with others. This will affect valuable sources of finance, meaning your creditors and maybe your bankers. Most businesses would find the demand of COD or prepayment difficult to withstand.

32. Company Funds vs. Personal Funds

Many ventures would succeed (even though some might not excel) simply by paying close attention to details and applying discipline.

I have seen small-business operators take money from the till to pay for personal services and not bat an eye, much less replace the money. This is a recipe for trouble.

Separating the business from the owners is a good way to leave the business's resources, particularly cash, for the purposes of the business.

This is not an issue of morality; it is about organizing in order to operate and understand what is going on. After all, if the businessman is the sole owner, he cannot really steal from himself.

The situation is compounded when the business has multiple owners who might operate the same way. One can easily see the confusion that can come from such a free-for-all, not to mention the issues of trust that may arise.

The small-business owner should pay himself and get extra funds via formal loans or dividends.

In some businesses that are not incorporated, there is a provision for a "drawings account" that allows for the orderly movement of funds for personal use. The owner can take money at any time, but there is a record of it, so the business accounts for the use of all funds.

Any other approach will create problems with the profit and loss statements and balance sheets, at the very least.

Small-Business Summary

Respecting the fact that the company's money is not personal funds is a good guide to maintaining proper administration, financial records, and general order. If the businessman keeps this in mind at all times, his general management will benefit from this discipline.

33. Selling to Your Friends and Relatives

Many small-business operators are happy to have made the plunge into the world of business. Even happier, sometimes, are friends and family—proud to have a businessman in the family at last.

Sometimes, in order to demonstrate this status as "a businessman," operators feel compelled to give some of their products free of charge to family and friends, or if they do sell them the products, they are not aggressive in collecting. They feel self-conscious about asking for the money, and the friends and relatives believe that refusing to collect is a gesture of kindness. Compound this with the possibility that the business offered a friendly discount in the first place, and this is bad for business.

If you would not do it for a stranger, it is probably bad for your business. Favors to friends and relatives should come out of salaries and dividends paid to you, which is your personal money. The key is to manage your resources so that the business is run efficiently and you can splurge with the profits.

This issue is not always easy to face in the real world. The key is to do your best and be aware of the pitfalls.

Many times, decisions in this regard are made in ignorance of their impact, but friends and family should be made to understand. Or, if they don't accept your decision, you have to decide what is important for the viability of the business.

Small-Business Summary

The impact of failing to collect from your friends and relatives is the same as not collecting from strangers. It is good to be aware of the difficulty beforehand so that you can minimize potential conflicts between those close to you and your business objectives.

34. Taxes

There are several types of taxes. One type is collected as a percentage of the value of the goods or service—basically a sales tax. Another type is collected from employees by the firm, where applicable. A third type is that which is due as a percentage of profits, also where applicable.

In all cases, the money is being collected on behalf of some aspect of government. It is not owned by the business but can provide some cash flow until it is due for payment, usually by a specific time of the month or year.

Many businesses run into problems if these funds are not properly factored in to their plans and paid when due.

The small business is especially vulnerable to this because of loose systems and/or cash flow constraints. The resulting penalties can be challenging.

Small-Business Summary

Taxation levied on the new business can be onerous and sometimes unreasonable, yet the penalties might be worse. Some jurisdictions might offer tax breaks and incentives, but in all cases, strive to be on the right side of the law as the penalties can be more disruptive than the taxes themselves.

SECTION IV

35. The Importance of Good Record-Keeping

Sometimes record-keeping gets in the way of running a small business. As discussed in an earlier chapter, I do not think that an entrepreneur should become bogged down with accounting issues too early because it is a technical area, and if he or she becomes overwhelmed with accounts, it can lead to discouragement. But I am not implying that accounts are not important. Proper accounts present an organized structure for analyzing progress. The question is: who should spend the time doing them?

Many businesspeople, old and new, are sloppy in this area, and it is to their detriment. The entrepreneur might buy goods and services for the business and may or may not keep his or her bills. He or she may sell the products and not store the invoices properly. Later, he or she has to show some proof of his or her activities and then seeks to reclaim and reconstruct. This wastes time, is inefficient, and can get him or her into legal and other problems.

Fortunately, there are simple accounting programs nowadays that can help you avoid such errors. Additionally, employing someone to update the system and categorize and store information can be easy and low-cost. By talking to friends and colleagues, you can get many leads about reasonable people offering accounting services part-time. It is worth the effort.

In these modern times, there is hardly any excuse for poor record-keeping, including catastrophes like fires, because information can be stored easily and safely by employing backup systems.

Refusing to invest in appropriate record-keeping is not a good way to seek cost control or savings.

Small-Business Summary

Formalize your record-keeping and administration as quickly as possible. Ultimately, this will save time and provide the best information on your progress for stakeholders.

36. Insights into Financial Statements

Take a survey of reasonably successful small-business people and see how many of them understand financials well, or how many started out understanding them well. The result would be a surprisingly low percentage. So, how well should you understand the financial aspect of a business before you start?

The August 20, 2009, issue of *Inc.* magazine reviewed a study undertaken by retail chain ACE Hardware. Of five hundred small-business owners surveyed, 79 percent had at least some college education, but only 7 percent thought it important to be educated in business or finance. The respondents listed the characteristics they thought to be important to entrepreneurial success as: industriousness, motivation, perseverance, intelligence, good instincts, and passion, in decreasing order of importance.

One can argue about the true list or the relative importance, but this information resonates well with the general theme of this book—in spite of their importance to business, knowledge of accounting and the ability to understand financials take a back seat to common sense and enterprise when operating a small business.

Financial statements are very important tools for evaluating business progress and success. Most stakeholders are supplied these statements from time to time. Bankers need them, and, not least of all, the shareholders (those who understand them) will want to monitor their investments via these tools.

Yet, they are not everyday documents and do not tell very much about how to deal with, for the most part, the "jungle" that is the business environment. An exception to this might be the cash budget or cash flow statement, which can be useful for daily or other periodic monitoring of cash.

So, what are these statements? Let's briefly consider three of the more important ones.

The profit and loss statement (often called P&L) is a summary account used at the end of a specific period to show the net result of the business's activities—whether the business made a profit or a loss. This is what one would show to a banker, a shareholder, or the taxman to indicate what profits have been made.

The period under consideration can be a week or any other amount of time, but it is typically a month, quarter, or year. Most records will list the month being considered against the corresponding month for a period in the past, for example, March 2009 versus March 2008.

Profit & Loss Statement (P&L) for the XYZ Company
Fiscal Year 2007 and 2008

Figures (USD)	2007	2008
Sales	370,000	400,000
Cost of Goods Sold (COGS)	(70,000)	(75,000)
Gross Profit	300,000	325,000
General Operating Expenses (R&D)	(35,000)	(40,000)
Depreciation	(12,000)	(12,000)
Operating Income	183,000	273,000
Other Income (Interest Income)	8,000	12,000
Extraordinary Income	—	(3,000)
Earnings Before Interest & Tax (EBIT)	191,000	282,000
Interest Expense	(10,000)	(10,000)
Net Profit Before Taxes (NPBT)	181,000	272,000
Taxes (10%)	(18,100)	(27,200)
Net Profit After Taxes (NPAT)	162,900	244,800
Dividends Paid to Shareholders	—	(20,000)
Retained Earnings	162,900	224,800

Figure 1: Sample Profit and Loss Statement

Why might you need to see comparable periods? Such comparisons will show how the business progressed. For example, a 12 percent increase from one year to the next might indicate good steady growth, whereas growth of 150 percent from one year to the next will indicate fantastic but perhaps unsustainable growth. Or, it might indicate unusual activities that led to this growth but that will not be repeatable. For example, a small business got a contract to provide services for the army during a brief period of war and the war is now over. Clearly, the management cannot plan to repeat this feat the next year.

Conversely, profits might fall dramatically following a previous year because the economy went into recession and the business's main clients or industries have been adversely affected.

The P&L takes into consideration all the costs and expenses associated with the business and all the revenues generated by the business. If there is more revenue than expenses, there is a surplus or profit, and if there is less revenue than expenses, there is a shortfall or loss.

A loss is not necessarily a sign of failure (also, try to minimize the idea of *failure*, as it can create mental stumbling blocks). At start-up, the business might need to spend a little more than it earns, but this is usually a necessary part of the building process.

Note, though, that the firm should aim to make profits well beyond the inflation rate. A company that made $100,000 last year and $101,000 this year, against the background of inflation at 10 percent, might be considered to have underperformed because the reduction in value of the money based on inflation means the firm's profits have not kept up with the required purchasing power to offset that inflation.

Oftentimes a business will not have "enough" money available. Yet it can continue to operate successfully and efficiently. This is because most money going out as expenses can be planned or known (for example, we need to pay wages on day twenty-five of each month). Additionally, when we sell, we know that 50 percent of the sales go out COD and the other 50 percent go on thirty days' credit. If customers usually pay on time, we can estimate and plan to receive money in time to deal with the need for money to go out. A cash budget helps to do this.

Note that there is both a cash flow statement and a cash budget. The two are similar. The cash flow statement is one of the three primary financial statements that give managers an indication of what is happening. Specifically, it tracks the movement of cash and helps to fill in the gaps about how money is moved around the business in terms of cash, investments, payments, receipts, etc. Activities will involve movements in two or all three of the statements, but the cash flow document—whether in the form of a cash flow statement or a cash budget—is the best reminder that profit is not cash and that cash can run out and create crises in spite of the business reporting profits. Conversely, cash can be available even while the firm is making a loss, although such circumstances are ultimately unsustainable.

The cash budget is more a forecasting type of document that shows how we expect cash to flow in all angles of the business. It should warn us of the need for cash, the likely timing of those needs, and what deficits might arise. It can also indicate surplus so we can plan to move money into short-term investments and not have too much lying around idly in low- or zero-interest accounts. Therefore, the cash budget is more relevant to the context of this book.

SIMPLE CASH BUDGET FOR A MONTH

USD		$
Beginning cash balance		32,000
Add		
	Estimated collections on accounts receivables	75,000
	Estimated cash sales	25,000
		132,000
Deduct		
	Estimated payments on accounts payables	80,000
	Estimated cash expenses	15,000
	Contractual payment of long-term debt	15,000
	Quarterly dividends	5,000
		115,000
Estimated ending cash balance		17,000

Figure 2: A Simple Cash Budget

Figure 2 shows a simple cash budget indicating the balance between expected inflows and outflows. In this case, there is an expected $17,000, showing a positive cash balance when all inflows and outflows are considered. The business can decide to invest this balance in a short-term savings instrument, make an extra loan payment, or pay some dividends to the shareholders.

If the business is having a tight balance between inflows and outflows, the statement is a very good management tool for monitoring and planning for cash needs.

So, if money typically comes in around the last week of the month, and if there is little cash available in the third week, that might not be a cause for alarm because the cash budget statement will show money coming in soon.

But, if there is cause for concern about cash availability, the cash budget statement serves another useful purpose. It allows the management to know ahead of time what is likely to happen and to take proactive steps. For example, it can start to negotiate loans and overdraft facilities with bankers or payment delays with creditors. These actions are taken to bridge the gap.

The cash budget statement serves yet another useful purpose. It demonstrates the relationship between profit and cash. When you get into business, you will come across an interesting concept: there is a difference between "profits" and "cash."

Making a profit does not mean that the firm collected money, and having a loss does not mean the firm does not have cash available.

This notion can be confusing to the new entrant into business; as I will explain below, at the start, try not to get caught up with understanding everything included in this idea. These ideas are used most productively by a businessperson who has had experience with them or someone like an accountant who is paid to understand and communicate these situations.

Please do not be daunted or deterred by financial statements; they will be made clear very quickly as you progress.

A balance sheet is defined as a statement of financial position at a particular date.

Your business will own things. These might be buildings, cash, money (also called "accounts receivables," which are considered yours even if they have not yet been paid to you), etc. These things are assets, and there are numerous types.

Conversely, the business might have to pay out (accounts payables). Accounts payables do not belong to you and are to be paid at some time. The things you need to pay for are termed "liabilities," and there are several types.

The balance sheet lists and summarizes the position of assets against liabilities and can state the net position.

If there are more liabilities than assets, it means bad news for the business.

SIMPLE BALANCE SHEET

	2008	2007
Assets		
Current assets		
Cash in hand	1,500.00	1,300.00
Cash in bank	3,200.00	3,475.00
Accounts receivable	2,600.00	2,500.00
Inventory	4,500.00	5,000.00
Prepaid expenses		
Rent	1,500.00	1,450.00
Total current assets	13,300.00	13,725.00
Fixed assets		
Equipment and fixtures (less depreciation)	1,500.00	1,400.00
Total assets	14,800.00	15,125.00
Liabilities		
Current liabilities		
Accounts payable	1,500.00	1,680.00
Notes payable (bank loan)	1,700.00	1,750.00
Accrued payroll expenses	400.00	350.00
Total current liabilities	3,600.00	3,780.00
Long-term liabilities		
Notes payable, 2012	4,500.00	4,500.00
Total liabilities	8,100.00	8,280.00
Net worth	6,700.00	6,845.00

*Net worth = Assets – Liabilities

Figure 3: Simple Balance Sheet

So there you have some simple but important information on the financial aspects of business. These statements have to be interpreted with caution and informed analyses. The data they contain have to be assessed by referring from one to the other and from one period (year) to the next.

To make matters more interesting, the data in the financial statements can be assessed by way of ratios. Simply, one gets a ratio by dividing one number into another. However, in the case of standard financial ratios, there is a certain type of number (for example, the net profit) that has to be on top and another type (for example, the total sales) at the bottom. That way, there is consistency in making comparisons, allowing everyone to assume that they are relevant and applicable.

To help explain this, consider a soft drink that is made from one hundred cups of water and five cups of corn syrup and an amount of flavoring that is effective but of negligible measurement. That approximates to 105 cups of soft drink. The ratio of water to corn syrup is 100/5, or 20. Another soft drink might have one hundred cups of water and ten cups of corn syrup, having a ratio of 100/10, or 10. The latter drink can be deemed sweeter by comparison (less water to syrup) simply by looking at the ratio and without tasting it.

Now, if we consider a business that had sales of $1,000,000 and made a profit of $2,000, it would have a profit-to-sales ratio of 2,000/1,000,000, or 0.002. The next year, the firm sells $2,000,000 and makes $2,000 profit. This is the same amount of profit, but this time, the profit-to-sales ratio is 2,000/2,000,000, or 0.001. Even with the same amount of profit, the previous year is deemed more profitable or more efficient. This is because during the previous year, the same profit was earned with lower sales.

One can develop a feeling of excitement with this information because truly committed small-business owners will start to glean ways to approach their businesses as a result of it. As you gain in experience, you learn how to make the ratios work out in your best interest. The information is very useful, but it requires either intuition or strong common sense to handle without some experience.

Thinking about the financials reminds me of a visit to the doctor. As standard procedure, they take one's blood pressure, temperature, and weight. These results can be "normal" and still not indicate potentially serious problems. This is also the case in financials. The usual ratios and other relationships might have to be assessed one against the other to make some good interpretations. For example, you might have high inventory turnover (indicating you are selling your stocks fast) because of too-low margins, making the products too cheap and ending up with too little profits.

Hence, financials do not necessarily show the pathway to growth. And they are historical, meaning that they are past data and do not necessarily reflect the present or forecast the future.

In spite of the views expressed about the financials in general, early focus on cash flow is important.

Daily attention to cash movements might be necessary, especially when finances are tight and there is a resulting need to preempt shortfalls and take action. This is accomplished by a cash budget.

Financials can be confusing, and the subject is more varied and involved than can be addressed in a few pages. It is how the subject is handled that makes the difference.

But the good news is that this is one of the easiest skills to buy. Accounting software and even a part-time accountant can make this information easy to acquire.

Throughout this book, we take a look at some of the other (numerous) factors that can make or break a small business. These "other factors" are attitudinal and involve insights and people skills. It is with these perspectives—in combination with financial information—that some very special things happen.

Small-Business Summary

It is important to understand what appears to be conflicting information on the views on and approaches to the financials. They are important, but understanding the business—the customers, products, and competition—will have more of your attention in the first two years. Without strong emphasis on these, the financials might be reporting "empty" information.

37. Getting Cash

How much cash do you need?

What type of financing do you need, and do you prefer debt (borrowing from an institution) or equity (getting money from others and giving up some ownership)?

Start-up costs are hard to pin down. The truth is that you might never get a full picture of what your needs are. Or you might choose to ignore some possibilities out of fear of the unknown, laziness, or unrealistic considerations.

If you need a computer that costs $1,500, but your brother promises to lend you one, then still factor in the cost of $1,500. If you manage to get the loan of the computer, your cost outlay will be less by that amount. That approach might be better than seeking an inadequate amount of money and then getting involved in a quarrel with your brother two days before the opening or that important trade show and having him withdraw his offer. Budgeting for the $1,500 helps to avoid a crisis if such a problem arises.

There are many pitfalls that you can encounter when looking at start-up costs. The first thing that I do is start a list. List as many possible considerations in getting your venture started as you can think of. It is better to have too many instead of too few.

A brainstorm can be helpful, too, because sometimes you are so excited about the prospects that you neglect some things that did not come naturally to your mind or that you pushed out unconsciously because they made you feel uncomfortable.

Examples of this are numerous. There are unsavory aspects in everything we do. For example, I do not like interviewing people, and therefore, I feel a subtle pressure to get the process going and over with. That can make me downplay the need to have an extra round of interviews and pay the attendant costs. There is a cost for doing them, and there is a cost for not doing them. The latter is a risk of poor performance.

A very important exercise that will take significant time is to estimate your future income, expenses, and cash flow needs. This is critical. You may have a very promising venture that requires a significant cash outlay, but it fails because you do not have enough to pay within the first few months that you are building the foundation.

This is why loan organizations will demand realistic cash flow projections. I recall an institution that was processing a loan for us. The projection showed the business running out of cash in the second year. The organization was demanding, and the loan was needed urgently. We were a bit sloppy in our preparation, and the lesson came home quite strongly.

If you are going to run out of cash so quickly, it means the venture might not be viable or that you need to show how you are going to fill the gap—perhaps via another loan from elsewhere.

Neither of these options will be welcomed by the primary loan institution, and in any event, you should not be encouraged to go down the wrong path.

The document is called a cash flow projection, but very often, specific implications pertaining to the flow are left out. To be considered is the flow of funds, or, rather, how funds flow based on the nature of the business or industry. The expected credit terms must be included from two industry-specific perspectives: what credit terms you expect to get and what credit terms you expect to give.

To illustrate this point, note that our chemical distribution company grew out of an investment of under $2,500. We cannot claim to have paid all our creditors on the specific due dates, but our record is such that they all give us a good report and there has never been a bank overdraft.

The reason for our initial success was that we got "cash" from suppliers—mainly our main supplier. We got terms of trade of thirty days' credit for 50 percent of the invoice and the other 50 percent payable in sixty days. We were then able to sell the products to large clients who paid in fifteen days. In fact, one of them had the practice of batching the invoices so that those not yet due were included in the payments.

This good fortune helped us to build a foundation, even though the lack of capital had other implications. I want to tie this in with my general tune throughout this book—that is, encouraging you to make your decision and take action. Not to move against good, sound advice but to take action knowing solutions are available to make success possible. Our business would not have passed any cash flow analysis, and to be fair, much of this was done in the early months without our taking a salary. But everyone who provided goods and services was paid, and interestingly, in an environment of slow economic growth, many were bemoaning receivables woes, but we had insignificant bad debt issues.

So, a cash flow projection would factor in, in our case, the reality that we were getting generous credit and giving limited credit. This resulted in a good cash position in which to grow with minimum capital injection of formal financing.

To underscore the impact of your approach and mind-set, let me tell you about a large company that had a monopoly selling a product for the construction industry. This firm faced competition only when it could not fulfill the market demand, because there was government control. The firm negotiated up to ninety days' credit from major suppliers and had preferential loan arrangements in many cases. It supplied some of its distributors on prepayment terms, meaning that the customer had to pay in advance, and I think there might have been some COD sales. Yet the company managed to get into bankruptcy and was bought out and the management changed. Thus, this near-ideal cash flow framework did not guarantee success.

These two contrasting examples might cause you to challenge the principle of the cash flow statement, but they should not. It is the mind-set, sense of purpose, and intent that will make the big difference. Many pioneers came to America hardly able to afford the boat fare. They soon carved out their piece of the pie without a cash flow statement. But their successful businesses subsequently learned to implement it.

So, since it is better to have a structure and to have a plan, here are some other things that you should consider in figuring your costs, including the expected incomes and how soon you might be able to move prices. How will inflation affect the price you will pay for your goods and services? The expenses include any benefits you will have to pay for employees—health insurance, uniforms, bonuses, etc. Consider utility and transport charges, finance fees, and bank service charges, if applicable. What about bad debt and other collection challenges? What are the taxation charges? In some cases, employers have to make compulsory payments on behalf of—and because of—staff. Consider capital expenses to get equipment and also working capital needed to deal with day-to-day expenses leading to the production and sale of the goods, including marketing costs.

There are more possibilities. Not all will apply to all situations, and some are not significant at start-up. But the need for cash and understanding how it flows are universal.

If the operator can get a loan, that can help. This is the typical way to go about funding a business. In this regard, some people have an almost fanatical attraction or aversion to one or another type of loan institution. Such preferences are a waste of time in many cases.

If you need money and your business can afford to get funding from an institution, simply select the one that will cost you the least and get on with the business.

Many businesses fail because of undercapitalization. Still more struggle because they cannot access affordable sources of finance. Some people simply will not qualify for loans regardless of the institution they try.

But entrepreneurship is about enterprise and imagination. Here are some ideas that have worked when traditional ones failed.

Consider whether there might be an insurance policy with some cash value that you can get or against which a loan can be taken. If there is money, you would be entitled to it.

Another avenue that can help is credit cards. One can get up to ninety days' credit from some suppliers, and paying off the supplier by credit card can achieve another thirty days or so. Yet, credit card juggling requires discipline. I have seen big interest payments resulting from the cardholder's waiting just one day beyond the due date and/or paying off the balance less a few dollars. Credit card interest rates are usually high, and many people cannot avoid the pitfall of frivolous spending. Beware!

Another source of funds is the so-called angel investor. Many people will invest in a start-up or going concern (that is, a business continuing its operations for the foreseeable future) with the expectation of a good return via interest or equity.

Be wary of people who seek to provide cash, expecting a return without operational involvement. You can find yourself with someone else's cash and work like a dog on his or her behalf.

Many friends and relatives have played a role without seeking to benefit beyond repayment, but oftentimes that approach presents a strain on relationships. Sometimes the timing for payback is not in sync with the needs, and sometimes the money is lost entirely. Business has risks.

You might get up one day and find that the bank has eliminated your line of credit, and even if you still have credit cards, their rates may start to get unbearably high. In a tight market, you could be working to pay interest only.

Many times bankers set stringent conditions for business owners to meet (including credit history) in order for the business to get a loan. This provides challenges for those with poor credit history. However, opportunistic money-lending firms will focus more on the company's assets (or its owners' assets) and its cash flow. If you have high sales volumes and low prices, your market risks are reduced because the sales revenues are less threatened, making your loan more likely to be approved. However, such loans are usually payable within a year, rates are high, and some places will require repayment frequencies as often as weekly to protect their interest. This can help to assure payments but might be demanding on the business.

Be careful of deals and agreements signed. A small fledgling business is unlikely to be able to pay the operator properly and pay exorbitant rates to others at the same time. The reality is that if you need cash and have few choices, the more desperate you seem and the more vulnerable you will be. Be wary of those who come bearing financial "gifts."

Yet another option of financing is called factoring or invoice financing. This involves selling your invoices or receivables to a third party at a discount. The discount is usually 5 to 10 percent of the face value. The factorer (the one making the purchase) makes money by collecting from your customers, requiring them to be of good quality—meaning that they will pay.

Another spin is that if you have inventory of a certain type—for example, raw material in high demand—you can borrow using the inventory as collateral.

These ideas and approaches are all products of creatively coming to a win-win situation out of necessity. The reason there are so many (and the list is far from exhaustive) is that, from time to time, people got into binds and thought creatively. Your circumstance, location, resources, and creativity will determine your needs and options.

Small-Business Summary

Getting cash can be challenging but necessary. I have had interesting experiences with it. One time, we could not move until a loan was in place, and in another case, we went in on a tight budget and limited resources. The realities set the stage. For instance, if expensive capital equipment is required, there is no easy way around that and there are fewer options. If you can get credit and effective financing via the trade (trade credit), then that can be an asset, too.

As in most business circumstances, much thought must be put into the deliberations driven by the realities of the business's needs, financing options available, personal resources, etc.

38. Controlling Costs

Controlling cost is, of course, one way of optimizing cash.

Very often people underestimate the amount of cash they need, especially if the business doesn't seem to be capital intensive. They also overestimate the speed with which revenue will come in. But surprises can lurk in the shadows.

Avoid unnecessary costs, especially at start-up.

Resist the fancy office or the fancy car. This can be difficult if one is coming from such roots. Believe it when I say that things have changed from the large office and BMW that the big company maintained on your behalf.

Such things as advertising can be "nice" but actually turn out to be unproductive costs. Many small-business people have been cajoled into finding an advertising budget by exuberant ad agents who do not even understand business basics.

In the most efficient approach, most advertising is wasted. Since one cannot easily discern which portion is wasted, most small businesses need to take good care to decide what is necessary to try and why.

Other areas of marketing are important. For example, you might have to spend on distribution activities, promotions, etc. However, these activities must be easily justified.

Astute marketing and sales activities should be designed to bring in cash.

There are many opportunities to monitor your costs. But first you have to understand them, know how they come about, and know what control you have over them.

I suggest that you sit with your accountant or an experienced businessperson and explain that you want to get a grip on your costs. Your motivation is different from the accountant's. You, as the general manager, need to figure out the why, and the accountant can help with the how.

If you use accounting software, it might summarize the costs, allowing you to see the overall effect. For instance, when you see a line on the report called "marketing" or "advertising," you can click on it, and it will open up a number of accounts showing the different categories and transactions that led to the final figure. You might be surprised how much you actually spend on some of these things, how controllable they might be, and how they change from period to period.

When you have a grasp of all your costs, you can discuss with the experienced person what they mean and how you can control or avoid them. When you look at each and compare them with other periods, you can see how they are changing and get insights into how you can influence them consciously. Here are some costs and issues that are sneaky and might surprise you, whether with their lack of control or their ability to get more cash flowing in:

1. The details of cash management. What do you do with excess cash? How can you do better with short-term investments? Do you have too many bank accounts costing you service charges, etc.?
2. Are you paying too much interest, and can you negotiate it?
3. Are you getting the best terms from suppliers? Can you get better terms and more credit and discounts?
4. Are you racking up bad debts, leading to penalty and other finance charges?
5. Can you lease equipment, even in the short term, so you can reduce initial capital outflows?
6. Can you reduce credit periods to customers, thus reducing the length of time money is on the road?
7. Can you improve your collection processes so you can get cash in faster?
8. Can you charge for deliveries where they have previously been free of charge?
9. You can change your buying pattern. If feasible, change from bulk purchases to more frequent, smaller purchases, or vice versa, depending on your production realities.
10. Are quality issues driving up your costs—reworking costs, returns, rejects, loss of customers, etc.?
11. Select and review credit customers carefully.

12. Tie commissions paid to collections and give salespeople a motive for maximizing their receivables management.
13. How about travel expenses—are they necessary and optimized?
14. Do you monitor and control office supplies and utilities? Are there opportunities for recycling? (We use the back of scrap prints and photocopies as informal notepads.)
15. Can you get multiple quotes for items before making a selection? Caution: This can be time-consuming, and you can get lower quality based on price. Sometimes you do not get the exact equivalents and, again, quality suffers.
16. What training is necessary to make staff more effective in carrying out the improvements?
17. Is training and motivation optimum to ensure process and administrative efficiencies?
18. Can you subcontract out work to save on having to prepare to do this work, or can you accept work in order to use spare capacity?

Many of these areas will be shown in the accounts; it just requires some time to identify and ponder them a bit.

The main approach of the small business should be lean and mean. Start with a modest salary. If possible, pay yourself and others a commission only for business brought in and place emphasis on variable costs as opposed to fixed costs. Generally, output will rise as variable costs rise, and this correlation should not be a problem. Use contracted workers if possible, but be prepared to share the profits if your penny-pinching pays off.

Small-Business Summary

Pinch on company costs and spend your personal money emanating from your investment as you like. If you pinch in the business and pinch on spending money on your family, you should wonder if your hard work is worth it. And, in spite of the need to control business costs, do not be driven to pinch your way into being ineffective. Some things are just worth your investment, and the question to consider is not whether you can afford it but if it is worth it—that is, does the expense provide commensurate value?

39. Accounting Concerns

You do not have to get bogged down by accounting issues too early. In the first year, a small business that is trying to seize the marketing initiative can lose sight of what leads to growth. Aim to avoid becoming overwhelmed by too much information, especially when you are not ready.

Let's say you have a great idea, but someone suggests that "management" requires understanding accounts. You try to understand formal bookkeeping and financial management, but it is boring, distracting, or confusing. So you register in a course or agonize over some self-training book that weighs you down and sends the message that this "thing" called business is difficult.

Most of the obstacles and apprehensions in business are self-imposed.

Certain businesspeople are not more successful than others simply because they are brighter. And the degree of success is not an indication of how much brighter one is in relation to another.

To illustrate this, consider Bill Gates of Microsoft. Let's say he has fifty billion dollars in wealth ($50,000,000,000). Now let's say that an average person has $50,000. If this were a proportional relationship, one might say that Bill Gates is one million times more capable than the average guy. But that seems unreasonable.

Bill Gates might have special skills and talents, but, most important, he knows what creates success and gets going on those things. He employs a lot of talent that addresses what he cannot or does not like to address.

Let's say you are an average person struggling with the subject of financials, and let's look at how you could proceed from a practical angle. You have an idea for a business. Do not first consider what you have to learn and what things are difficult. First share the intention with a trusted adviser, mentor, or anyone who is able to give good feedback and advice. Share what you want to accomplish, depending on how much information you feel comfortable passing on. Make a start.

The person, especially one with insights and experience relevant to your project, will provide revealing information and angles. A trusted adviser who runs a business might even provide some access to his or her accounting staff to walk you through the process, give you advice, or otherwise help you weigh the options.

If the project is deemed feasible, most of the effort should focus on learning about how to make the idea relevant to the real marketplace and how to sell the market its value. In the first year or so, this is where the attention should be placed.

But from day one, you should develop a disciplined approach to your accounts. In this regard, you should use accounting software and hire (particularly part-time) help to develop and keep your records, interpret the statements, and give advice.

I know someone who had an opportunity to buy a small confectionary business at a good price. The person was flustered by the prospects of owning and running a business, especially as she had no intention to leave her current job. She spoke with the general manager of a firm selling sugar, and he put her in touch with a firm that had factory space to rent. He also helped with brainstorming ideas and offered the assistance of his financial partner, who helped to develop the business plan and set up the accounts using packaged software.

The business was up and running within months, and the adviser's company supplied the sugar. (This is a good example of a win-win situation, but advisers do not necessarily need business or payment in return.) The owner soon had the time to understand the intricacies of financial management.

Small-Business Summary

Try to keep in mind that these ideas are meant to get to the heart of the issues, and simplicity can be effective. The intention is not to oversimplify but instead to counter the tendency to overcomplicate things. I have seen nearly illiterate people start and run small businesses successfully, and this supports my claim that the significant processes take place in the mind.

40. Seek Mentorship/Coaching

Do you know one person who can change your life for the better? Someone who can help to ease your stress and anxieties by sharing his or her experience? Someone who has done something close to what you are trying to do and is prepared to assist you?

The relationship you need might not be formal, in the sense that it is contractual or has specific schedules. If you can find people who have experience and have been a success in any type of business venture, usually they are glad to share with you.

So try to surround yourself with people who believe in you and your goals. If you have a number of people who come together for your cause, some might refer to this as a mastermind group. However, you have to stay in control because it is your idea, your intention, and your plan.

Bear in mind that some people will be genuinely interested in assisting you but lack the depth or ability to offer useful assistance.

An example of this occurred when one of my colleagues went to a deacon of his church for assistance. They normally discussed personal issues, and my friend would get (usually spiritual) guidance. The deacon was kind and receptive, and each time they met, he offered prayer for the business, listened, and sought to make sure that my friend was acting with due respect to the wider Christian values. Yet, by nature, he was suspicious and conservative and knew almost nothing about running a worldly business.

Soon my friend was forced to confer with someone else—a person who was in business, having left a firm where he worked for fifteen years before the business went bankrupt. This other adviser had learned many things about cost control, budgeting, buying and selling within tight constraints, and other crisis management strategies. He was able to offer much more practical advice; in addition, since he was by then a small-business owner himself, he offered to share his office with my friend for a small fee. This proximity added even more value because my friend gained a useful resource situated just across from his desk.

You have to ask yourself who is most suited to be your mentor and where you can find him or her.

Interestingly, you will find that many times in your business (and life in general) the best things come for free. The evaluation of who is most suitable is not easy because what you need is value. As I have pointed out many times, most of the challenges you will encounter will involve your mind—how you perceive situations and how you respond to them.

I cannot tell you exactly how to go about getting a mentor. It depends. The person available and beneficial might be a member of your son's PTA. Knowing what he does, you can assess his personality (will he be personable and helpful?) and ask for assistance. If he is willing and has any experience or expertise in an area connected to your area of interest, then he could be your coach.

Wherever you are located, you might see indications of people who can help. There are people with problems that they have solved or problems that they need to solve (thus giving you possible opportunities) and people with insight, opinions, and suggestions that can be modified to fit your specific circumstance. We are always surrounded by such resources, but most times the signs are not necessarily clear. By becoming aware of their value, you can develop the ability to spot opportunities to get assistance in your venture.

One day I was standing in a line at the bank and overheard two men discussing their businesses. On the subject of sales reps' compensation, one said he paid a small percentage to salespeople, tied to their commission, for the purpose of customer entertainment. This avoided a fixed cost and encouraged some correlation between entertainment and performance. The other one suggested paying a small fee to reps to collect customer data. He used this data to update his database and ensure that he had continuity when reps left. Both ideas sounded novel, and I made notes to try some variations of them in my own business. I did not speak with them, but I could not help overhearing and got some free ideas. Help is available from unusual sources.

What about a formal process for getting mentors?

I entered "finding business mentors" in a Google search and got 12.3 million hits, including one that said, "The Mentors: Kent Sutherland solicited Wal-Mart's Sam Walton as his business mentor 18 years ago and has prospered ever since."

Of course, Sam Walton was the founder of Wal-Mart. Can you get someone of similar esteem to be your mentor? Everyone would pay dearly to get that caliber of mentorship. But the point I am trying to get across is that there is no magic, just intent. The guts to approach Sam Walton was the source of Kent's success, and I am not sure there is a formula to illustrate it. I am not saying there is no formal process for seeking mentors, but instead, I am emphasizing the importance of seizing the opportunity.

Some mentors and coaches advertise. Let's examine the possibilities of success with a mentor who advertises his or her services. Many are available via the Internet, and mentoring is their business. They solicit clients for mentorship. The various fees can run to thousands of dollars per hour or per person for seminars and events. There are mentors for almost any area of business—indeed, any area of life!

Seriously, though, what are the realistic expectations from a commercial mentor who contracts this way? For his or hers to be considered a viable business, the mentor must have several clients. For there to be value to the clients, the mentor must invest time, and each need is different. Who can spread himself or herself over all these possibilities and provide an assurance of quality, beneficial service to all?

I understand that some have a staff of assistants; the mentor uses his or her name (brand) to solicit business, and someone else handles the details... not necessarily what you paid for or what you expect because the professional mentor sold you on what *he or she* had accomplished. In the end, you can discern the value you expect and decide if taking this route is worth it.

The life of a small-business owner can be demanding, lonely, and frustrating. Not that the big-business owner does not have the same challenges, but generally, he or she does not have the resource constraints. Additionally, he or she tends to have a much bigger pool of people from whom to draw inspiration and advice. Indeed, he or she can pay whatever consultants come along.

The small entrepreneur has to develop a plan and a process to find successful people and learn from them. He or she must learn from people who lose, too. The idea of losing is given a bad name, but what it means, most importantly, is that the individual tried. Wouldn't it be good to know what to avoid? Sometimes you can learn more from losing than from winning because you do not always know why you won.

As soon as you start a venture, find someone who will share his or her experience and get the benefits of some fast-track experience. Most successful people have big egos and love to talk about their experiences. Some will be proud to talk about those they have helped to become who they turned out to be.

Good advice is not too scarce. And usually it is for free, except when it is over a meal or refreshment, which you should gladly pay for. Much of what is discussed in this book will also be the topics that a good mentor or coach will highlight.

Small-Business Summary

As soon as possible, find people, outside the business, who can give you objective advice and feedback on your plans and progress. Choose people not for emotional support but for guidance on how to do the things that will lead you to your desired results.

41. Employee Selection—Building Your Team

Harvey Mackay wrote that he would get out of business if he did not like the rigors of hiring properly. I sympathize with him. I am not sure about getting out of business voluntarily, but having a set of subpar employees will at best retard growth.

Blessed are those who have people who know what to do, know how to do it, and know when to do it. As a small-business operator, there is no better feeling than being assured that an employee can, and will, take care of business.

The rigors of selecting people can be rewarding. A bad selection can be devastating.

Even though there are no guarantees, please make some effort to select properly. It will be the single most important contributor to your growth! Know what type of people you need and what you will accept.

The small-business person, especially at start-up, might not have the time and resources to hire the best. The business usually starts off very informally, and many times the decisions are understandably made based on who is available and affordable. Just try to do your best in this area.

But some operators get this point better than others and creatively achieve success even with minimum resources. They do this by being aware of important strengths and focusing on these strengths when hiring. They then provide incentives to encourage the type of results they want.

Many times the small operator is without time and appoints an outside person or firm to do the selection. That can work, but it is expensive, and sometimes the fit into the particular business culture is not achieved or the operator still has to invest time to ensure that it is.

Warning! Be careful about employing friends and relatives. Firing them or demanding discipline can be a challenge. Most do not come with the maturity and integrity to deal with this potential conflict of interest.

Your team can comprise two sets of people: those you pay and those committed to your success for free. To help in selecting those you pay, you should define what you want the job to accomplish. If you need a secretary, decide if this is an assistant or someone who will respond to your every whim. As you are paying, you should call the shots, but there needs to be an understanding of what is expected from both sides. Sometimes a good, honest discussion of the job is necessary to achieve that.

In my case, once I leave home, I have had breakfast and do not require a beverage of any sort. Later, I need water and usually provide that for myself. Therefore, I never require someone to get me a drink. However, some people expect their assistants to get their coffee each morning. Some assistants will accommodate this expectation but do not like the role.

Very often the assistant in a small firm is a jack-of-all-trades and a valuable member of the team. No one likes to be taken for granted. Requiring certain roles can cause stress on the relationships. A small company may only be able to pay a fraction of their market value, and the need to fetch coffee makes them feel less than appreciated.

The small-business operator must be sensitive to this as many people will not complain openly and might become frustrated enough to leave. A good assistant or administrator is priceless to the small business. Some years ago, the office manager of a small business complained bitterly to me about one owner who had the habit of coming in from the heat of the day and routinely asking for a glass of water. The first time she got it as a favor and was not concerned. The next time she did it reluctantly, and thereafter, she slowly built up resentment against him until she left the job.

Consider another approach in which the business owner occasionally brings in a hamburger for the assistant and, when required, moves about the kitchenette with a sense of sharing. That sets the tone of teamwork, encourages the assistant to go the extra mile, and prevents apathy. Hence, when the assistant is required to stay into the night and when, as oftentimes happens in the early days, he or she is alone in the office for extended periods, the owner can be out seeking business without being too concerned.

For the small business, there might not be any advantage in applying an overkill hiring procedure, but consider these basic points to the approach. For each job, consider what you want to get done and the scope of the position. Look a little down the road and try to determine how the requirements might grow with expansion. Ask questions such as: What minimum qualification does the job require? What experience would be desirable? What skills are important or good to have? (Nowadays, computer literacy is important and a skill like Web site design might be good to have.) Where would you see the person being positioned in two to three years, and what kind of training program would help to take him or her there?

Psychometric testing, though not foolproof, can help to make a good personality fit, especially for demanding areas like sales.

Human resource issues are not my forte. I tend to depend on that elusive trait called "initiative." It is said that about 2 percent of people do not have to be supervised, and I like to think I am one of those people. Being highly analytical, I assess my situations and try to discern what is necessary to achieve the objective I seek. I try to get the knowledge that is required; hence, I will "take the initiative" to learn about my products as soon as I see that lack of such knowledge is hampering me. Yet some people will struggle with poor results and, without being sent to a training program, will not make the first move.

Since I depend on this elusive "initiative," I tend to seek out and like working with people who seem to have it as well. Yet other employers will be more successful by selecting with care and having a set of deliverables within the framework of a strong monitoring process.

Your staff needs to be monitored. Failure to monitor properly can result in an employee spending two years in a position and not growing in capability beyond the first month of employment.

If your small firm has four people and all are reasonably well suited for their roles and are developing within those roles, you can take it for granted that your firm is achieving.

The other part of your team comprises people who will help you (free of charge) for who you are and because of their commitment to your dream. This idea overlaps with the section on coaching and mentors, but the individuals do not have to play the part of organized help. Someone you meet routinely may be a part of your wider life outside the business and can make some contribution. Call up whomever you can and evaluate how, based on what they do and who they are, they can make a contribution to your success. See the section on mentoring to get ideas of what you can expect from a wider support group.

Small-Business Summary

Big companies become big as a result of how they organize their human resource selection and development. Building a good team and minimizing costs are especially important to the small firm when it gets going. It takes time and money to get good people, but it is a good investment. The challenges of economic uncertainties and other surprises are best handled with a team of capable and motivated employees who are dedicated to your cause.

42. Sales Rep Selection

Sales rep challenges surround one of the most vital parts of growth, if your firm depends on this resource.

Who is a sales rep? Many people will say that in the small business, everyone is a sales representative. That might be so anecdotally, but the business must have people who are charged with the frontline responsibility of selling. The role might be one of promoting, where, for example, everything is done online or in some other public media. Some salespeople are simply required to walk about, answering questions and giving advice. Others are placed in the field or on the telephone to be convincing and persuasive. For the latter, the job can be demanding and frustrating.

In any aspect of your business, sales rep selection and monitoring is demanding and requires a deliberative and purposeful individual or team to succeed—not just to get by.

I have conducted interviews and hired candidates within minutes because I find it difficult to be totally objective about this and it is a task I do not like. Hence, for me, the quicker it can be done, the better. Big mistake.

Who should do the selection? Should the manager do it?

It depends on the manager's skills and propensities for the task. If the manager cannot dedicate his or her full commitment, he or she should question whether he or she is suited. The job can be delegated or outsourced, but the person or people dedicated to the task should be able to fit the prospective employee with the company's needs and culture.

A truly small start-up will not have the luxury of a team, and the manager usually doubles as operations and marketing/sales manager. The two roles are seldom well handled by one individual. In fact, even marketing and sales can require separate and different personalities!

If you are not capable of being at least acceptable in sales management, get yourself an effective sales manager early.

What about the much sought-after experience? A person who claims to have sales experience because he or she was primarily doing customer relations activities in a big firm might waste your time. If he or she needs a job badly, chances are that he or she was doing poorly at that big firm.

I have had candidates for sales rep positions tell me how many millions in sales they had brought in at a previous job. In one example, it turned out that the performance was simply based on how the business grew when hardware stores bought stocks in an industry upturn. This had nothing to do with the sales rep.

Here is a point that took me a while to learn and accept: good, experienced sales reps are not generally attracted to small businesses. It might not fit their ego and esteem—two things necessary for their success in competitive selling. This has nothing to do with you or your firm, per se; it has to do with a simple fact of life. Even if the compensation is good, it might not appeal to them. Be wary of the salesperson who says he or she has decided to move a step down career-wise.

The general approach of getting a CV and deciding from it can be a waste of time. One of the best performing sales reps I have worked with was hired at start-up, when we did not have the time to request a CV. Later, when she was asked to bring one in, it was the worst document I had ever seen. On the other hand, one of the most suitable CVs I've seen came from a young lady who was very qualified and attractive on paper. She was hired in ignorance and could not sell anything.

Be careful about accepting CVs...and be careful about accepting references. They are usually supplied by candidates who have strong relationships with the people referring them. It's also possible that a person put down as a reference sees only the "positives" or, in any event, decides to paint a glowing picture of the candidate. In checking references, you should be astute in asking questions and be able to probe further into the referee's slightest hesitation or careful choice of words during the conversation.

The idea of hiring also brings me to a point of contention in sales: who are better at sales, men or women?

What I know is that selling is demanding, and the rep who shows application and discipline will win.

I know a male sales rep (now manager) who went into selling directly after leaving high school. He started in life insurance then switched to chemicals. He made a few mistakes, was corrected in his approach (by someone whom he later hired), and has done a fantastic job. He was a natural—hardworking, excited, motivated, smart, and successful. (Alas, these words do not describe most of those who have tried selling!) He is also one of the few reps who moved to sales management successfully.

Nowadays, you can dramatically improve your chances of success in selecting salespeople by using certain psychometric tools. These can help to take away the subjectivity and actually reduce the time involved. With such a tool, the small business can improve its chances by selecting not necessarily the most experienced people but even inexperienced people with the right selling personality.

This point took me a while to grasp because of the tradition of using CVs and hoping that the person would bring some "experience" from which we could benefit. Oftentimes what he or she brings is the baggage you want to avoid.

A young person who has a knack for sales might be groomed to grow in your small firm without the challenging issues of salary, image, esteem, etc. that the well-experienced person brings. Additionally, once he or she has what is called a "sales personality," the person will behave in ways that create success while building experience. Just provide an effective program to teach him or her product knowledge.

Even with the best efforts and selection processes, many will not like selling or be a good fit in your firm. The final advice in this situation is: terminate. And be quick!

This advice requires a mental toughness and determination to follow through, and most do not have this. We hope for another day, a better day; we hope that we will recoup all we have invested if we just give the salesperson another chance. But termination is the only way to deal with the problem.

If general employee selection is important, then sales rep selection is even more so—especially in these difficult times.

Truly, the only way to ensure that your organization will have an effective sales force is to select correctly and deal quickly with those who do not fit in.

Small-Business Summary

A salesperson's job can be as simple as answering the phone or as complex as having a territory to canvass. The full nature of one's selling needs and approaches will differ from business to business, but try to be very deliberate about how you assess what you need, who you will hire, and how you will monitor them. The further away the rep will operate outside of your scrutiny, the better he or she should be at selling. This assumes you know what to look out for. You should understand your business and the business environment to be able to make sense of reports and other feedback and what the sales data is saying. Any investment in developing a good sales team will pay off.

43. Time Management Awareness

The entrepreneur has many demands on his or her time.

Depending on the nature of the business, he or she can move from mopping the floor to negotiating with bankers, suppliers, or customers within minutes. The entrepreneur therefore has to plan for many situations.

Many books have been written on time management. The basic considerations like making lists and appointments, understanding your high-energy period of the day, and making use of some technology while avoiding others, like those focused only on entertainment, are fundamental. Subtler are the considerations that are necessary but require some discipline and intent to figure out.

For example, the business's main tool, a car, might be in need of significant service and attention but is still running. There can be a tendency to ignore the problem because of the two or three hours it requires to be fixed. Then, later, it breaks down on a lonely road, taking hours to get help and costing six times the original price to repair. Avoiding the necessary maintenance time is not a good approach to time management.

Then there are traffic issues. If traffic is a problem, try to move around outside of the times of peak traffic and/or make use of training or inspirational CDs while on the move.

Entrepreneurs need to consider such issues as health and take steps to avoid being unavailable due to sick days. Thus, try to find about one hour per day to dedicate to exercise. This advice might be ignored because of "lack of time." However, this effort should be seen as an investment to prevent time off for illness or doctor's appointments.

Thinking ahead, even about your parking, can save valuable time. I have an office in a small business complex. The parking there can be tight, and it is not unusual to see someone walking from office to office, trying to find the driver of a car that has blocked him or her in. This wastes much time.

I arrive early. It is amazing how much more you can get done by turning up early. I park, facing out, at the nearest exiting position with a minimum chance of being blocked in. When I get ready to leave, I am less rushed, less stressed, and do not need extra time to find some elusive car owner blocking my way. It is this kind of clinical approach to time management that can help to make the small operator succeed and to reduce stress.

A key to time management is the level of motivation one has to do tasks. Procrastination is the thief of time. Many tasks are unsavory and are therefore avoided. One of two approaches can make things easier, free up your time, and reduce your stress. Attempt the hard tasks first thing in the morning. Make that difficult call or have that demanding meeting. Then after that has been accomplished, your relief will propel you forward to the other things. Or you can do the simpler things first and have no choice but to move to the harder tasks. Personally, I prefer the former approach, but use whichever works better for you.

As stated before, you don't have a lot of time, but you can control how you spend the little time you have. A common mistake is for the small-business owner to be driven by a fear of failure or over-ambition. Because of the limited time resource, you have to see things in terms of what will be most productive and rewarding, and spend more time on those things.

The fear of failure goes away if you are focusing on what you want. Managing ambition will help you to understand that you cannot do it all by yourself.

If you review what motivated you to be in business and place that side by side with what you want to accomplish, you will find it easier to have a purposeful existence driven by what truly are your priorities. Taking this route provides more time, energy, and enjoyment in your business.

Once you have established the priorities, try to set up business processes to run themselves. Some things you cannot avoid because they are necessary for a modern business to run efficiently (these include invoicing activities, filing, marketing, letter writing, record-keeping, accounting, budgeting, planning, etc.).

See what areas can be outsourced, set up to run automatically, or otherwise taken from you to allow for a more fulfilling use of your time.

Small-Business Summary

There is a feeling of relaxation and productivity that comes with a rewarding use of your time. Because one cannot add more hours to the day, one has to "make time" by being efficient, effective, and purposeful. Identifying the thieves of your time is good, but organizing to eliminate them is better. That comes about by setting priorities based on a solid sense of purpose in your daily activities.

44. Patience

I learned an important lesson at about age nine or ten. My father had recently planted a coconut tree for me, and I asked him how long it would take to bear fruits. He said about seven years. To a nine-year-old, seven years seem like a lifetime. The planted tree was uprooted within a few days by some stray animal or something, and I didn't bother to have it replanted. It was going to take too long to develop anyway.

To this day, this incident still haunts me because all I had to do was replant the tree. That would have given me a lot of years to literally enjoy the fruits of my labor.

Coconut trees take time to develop, mature, and bear fruits. So do many businesses.

I think that success requires what I term "patient impatience."

A person who is studying to be a doctor cannot avoid some years of study. Yet within the period of studies, he or she can be wary of how he or she spends his or her time daily. The student doctor has to be impatient with anything that conflicts with the productive use of his or her time each day and be patient with the expanse of time necessary for qualification.

This is the same in business.

It takes time to set up a building, to do market research, to get financing, to get customers, etc.

But when these things are to be done, there should be no procrastination, no shifting of responsibilities, and no watching TV when serious work is necessary.

You have to be known as someone who takes *action*. Results require time. Time is an intricate part of the mix, and so the entrepreneur is advised to be realistic about time. Be patient but be useful. Move purposefully, and the results will come.

Small-Business Summary

In applying diligence to your efforts, you recognize that you need to be efficient and purposeful but that success requires time and the results will come once you have laid the groundwork.

45. Networking

Networking means different things to different people. To many, the idea of networking can be negatively perceived. Some see this as being false and sucking up to others, just in case (or by design) they might be able to do something for them later.

I know a sales manager who had an expense account provision. For nearly a year he did not use it at all; the business did not benefit from his proclaimed "networking skills" and "contacts," which were highlighted at the start. Yet, later, when he was assessed negatively, he defended his value by repeating his assertion that he could "open doors" for the firm. So, clearly, networking means different things to different people.

When a contact introduces you to another, for the purposes of exploring business, there is a better chance of getting business than from cold calling.

If you play golf at the same club or belong to the same lodge as a particular contact, you have a greater chance of securing his or her business. That is a simple fact of life. That is networking.

Many old boys' networks exist for the purposes of business development, and many people who purport to join "service clubs" for the community's sake have more than a few selfish reasons. But that, too, is life.

If your contact is owed a few favors, that can also create opportunities for you.

Organized networking is perhaps the best chance you have to make connections, build relationships, and get ahead. If you link with people with similar issues, problems, and outlooks, you can find many opportunities for answers and insights.

Start with a goal. Know what your objectives are in seeking a special group for the purpose of networking. You can expand your sphere of influence and become the person known for solving problems in a certain industry.

You can decide to be passive in that you listen and learn, or you can take a lead role, teach, and become known for your expertise.

Once you identify the ideal group for you, start by attending regularly and by offering free service and volunteering. This brings people to you, and the relationships can be tapped for mutual benefits.

By reading local newspapers and other community-based publications, you can find out where the action is. If you find a group that seems interesting, you can research them on the Internet or by asking people connected in some way, even beneficiaries of their services. If you have genuine questions on what they do, those can be discussion points to get you in communication and to help you feel more comfortable when you attend the first meetings.

Research topics pertaining to your niche. Write articles for newspapers and magazines. Make appearances on TV and radio programs, if you can. Many people have suddenly experienced mega-growth by simply (it seems) appearing on *Oprah*!

Depending on the group and what you find out, you can likely get more information from searching on the Internet. For example, you can check up on specific people of influence and join blogs or discussions so that you can be up to date with relevant issues.

It is a good idea to start off showing proper courtesies and manners regarding the communication process. Thank-you notes and answers to requests should be prompt. Any promise you make should be acted on, and explanations should suggest you know what you are talking about.

The guiding force for building a business should be a good base. Develop a good base of customers, satisfactory service, and a good spread of products to minimize risks. Make sure that networking highlights the tangible benefits that people will get from your services if they give you a chance.

As a final point (and warning) on this subject: Note how many businesses falter when some changes occur. A good example is on the political front. Significant opportunities can come via political contacts, but then, when politicians change, your business might be thrown out, too. This can happen with any organizational change. When personalities change, so might the businessman's fortunes.

Small-Business Summary

Broaden your outlook on networking. Organize with related businesses and with people who come into contact with your products or who need your products. A real estate agent, for example, might be dealing with clients who need cleaning chemicals. So, if you are in the chemical or cleaning business, you might get access to big buildings by networking with real estate agents. Once your name and reputation have gotten out and you are doing a good job, you will find business searching for you.

SECTION V

46. Choosing an Accountant

Accountants bring their personalities to their careers. Many are conservative and pay attention only to the technical details, leaving little room for the wider imagination and creativity a business generally needs. Some are disorganized, and even if they're smart, the business operator has to determine what is needed of them. Hence, as an entrepreneur, you have to know how much you can depend on your accountant.

Try to get one who is experienced and knows the law. See if he or she is prepared to sit with you and discuss your business, clarifying many of the nuances of the business, the financial information, and their impact on your viability and profitability.

Many times the small business's needs are pushed behind the needs of the bigger firms, not surprisingly, because the big ones might be making a bigger impact on the accountant's bottom line. Still, you are important, too, and should demand appropriate attention.

I have found that an accountant who started out with the challenges of building a business himself or herself can be of tremendous assistance in helping a small business understand the issues.

A good accountant and a good accounting system are invaluable. The accountant can assist with the choice of the best business structure—that is, whether to go the route of a partnership, sole proprietorship, or corporation. He or she can help with planning your capital needs, your accounting system, filing returns, interpretation of financial data, cash flow issues, budgeting, inventory management, and pricing. Even though the list seems long, many of these items are considered on a phased basis. For example, filing tax returns is generally at the back end, and some, like inventory management, are things that you tend to fine-tune as the business progresses.

A manufacturing venture might require more time and effort dedicated to costing than a simple distribution firm. The more inputs into the manufacturing process, the more effort required to get the numbers right.

Hence, variations in labor costs, raw materials, and processes can require more attention.

This could be daunting for the business owner. Even if you are an MBA graduate, there is a good chance that you will struggle with the initial stages of doing the "real world" work in determining your costs.

The best way to go about this is to outline the plan to your accountant. Based on the plan, the accountant will require some figures. He will let you know what these figures are, and you will provide them.

If you are going to open a restaurant, the numbers will be worked backwards and forwards. You will have a sense of what the various menus will cost and gain some expertise in the preparation of meals so that you can discuss the inputs in a practical way. Depending on your niche market, you can charge just so much for the food and remain in business. Also, your inputs will include agricultural produce, and the price of fresh produce can depend on the weather, among other things. So the accountant who understands how to do costing (and risk management) will have to be guided on the process so that he or she can apply the "what ifs" to the process.

During this process, questions and issues will arise that were not considered before because, after all, chances are that you either have not done business before or you have technical problems with some aspects of the business. The process, therefore, is a learning one. You will learn from the accountant, and he or she will learn more about some of the things that go into such an operation. It is in this way that you will truly become more enlightened about your business and how to get the resources you need to succeed.

If you take the traditional advice to "learn accounts" and "do your business plan," you might be confused, lose your motivation, and become despondent. Or you might go it alone, do the numbers incorrectly, and have unrealistic costs and prices.

Use the help of a friend or colleague to get the process started, if you can. I know someone who started a small business but who was lost regarding his costs and pricing. A friend recommended an accountant, and he helped to get the costing and other issues right for free, helped to set up accounting software, and then charged about $500 per month just to make sure things were going well, answer questions, and give advice. This was a simple operation, and soon the owner understood the financial issues better and better.

But what does an accountant cost? You can expect to pay about $150 to $400 per hour depending on the type of work. It also depends on the location. Routine work from people with limited experience will be cheaper, and the expertise you require depends on the stage of the business and the nature of the transaction.

Advice on how to do bookkeeping is simple and perhaps the easiest to buy. Acquiring a business is more complex than a new start-up and usually requires more time and money. The type of help you need depends on your industry and the complexity of the business, and it also depends on how much you understand about business and how fast and willing you are to acquire the requisite knowledge.

Our business used QuickBooks software and an accountant who helped to interpret the outputs. We got reasonably good monthly reports, and the formal annual audit uncovered necessary adjustments.

A good accountant will be able to provide invaluable guidance and advice. The numerous reports from the software can be overwhelming, but the accountant can help to make sense of them and to prioritize their use. In selecting the right accountant, you need to be comfortable with the relationship, and if the person has some experience in your industry, that is a plus. This requirement increases with the business's complexity.

For example, you might want to export or take advantage of some opportunities, tax incentives, etc., and the need to maneuver among the variables requires a knowledgeable person to advise you.

You will recognize that this process can be time-consuming and involve many factors. This fact underscores the point of this book. Instead of trying to cover every possible angle, it is more important that I get the main point across: there has to be sufficient commitment to your idea and business to bring out a "can do" attitude so that the answers will come. What happens if your budget cannot pay an accountant $400 per hour? Does that mean your venture will fail? Not necessarily.

The answer depends on the circumstances, but your attitude will determine the outcome—different outcomes for different circumstances. I have known an entrepreneur to get an accountant to convert 50 percent of his fees into a loan. The accountant's risk was that he would not get paid if the business did not work out. I have also seen an accountant make his prices very cheap because he needed to get his practice off the ground and build goodwill.

No one answer fits all.

Small-Business Summary

An accountant who can help you to build a good set of financials, records, and systems is invaluable. But depending on your background, training, and propensity for certain details, you can determine how to optimize the services of this resource. Remember, though, *you* run your business, and over-dependence on your accountant for general management is not practical.

47. Choosing a Banker

Commercial banks make funding decisions by placing a strong emphasis on the individual's ability to repay loans and less on the business plans presented. So do finance companies. The approach to financing in the formal sector has driven up the growth of unsecured loans in the less formal sector. This is widely applied in countries like Bangladesh and India.

There is a dynamic at play that ensures that opportunities meet preparedness. While the attitude of formal lenders might be an obstacle, many people have other avenues opening up for them. Many business ideas can withstand high interest rate repayment, while some cannot. Many people are so confident in their ideas that they will do anything for a chance to put them into action.

According to the *Financial Times* of February 2008, Bangladesh Grameen Bank became hugely successful by taking risks in lending to poor people in Bangladesh. Their huge success has encouraged the expansion of their pioneering micro-finance techniques to many people in richer nations; in particular, they have moved into New York, lending to people with no bank accounts.

Some countries are seeing private sector businesspeople borrowing the concept and filling a gap. The interest rates are very high, but for many, it is their only chance. Actually, many use these avenues for funding, and they are growing. The options depend on the laws, the stage of development, and economic policy (for example, is there an export drive that attracts government concessions; are there private sector initiatives; and what is the state of the economy?).

Ask yourself what opportunities there are and what options you can uncover. There are developments taking place over time (especially now, during the recession) that will create many changes, and taking a "can do" attitude will help to uncover these opportunities. The informal loans sector will evolve, and the formal sector will respond. What this should mean is greater opportunities for those with good ideas and plans and a good sense of commitment to them.

The small-business person needs to do business in several ways with banks but can feel ignored by the commercial bank, unless there is a personal relationship.

The small-business operator should make an effort to build a relationship with his or her bankers.

How else can he or she gain advantages, since his or her bank balance is not usually one that will command immediate attention?

Expanding this a bit, you also need to make friends with tellers and others at the clerical level. It is worthwhile to know that you can step into the bank on a Friday afternoon, near the end of the month, and not have to wait two hours in line. This is not to say you should be pushy, but as with most other things in life, it is he or she who has paved the way that will make the better trip.

The small-business operator, who is a jack-of-all-trades, sometimes needs to get back to the job and cannot afford to spend hours to do a one-minute transaction. Someone who will do him or her a favor from time to time is good to have. However, he or she should not abuse it.

Small-Business Summary

"Bankers" does not refer only to loan institutions but also to most financial institutions that help to streamline your financial activities. However, funding and interest rate issues will be high on the agenda of most small businesses, and the owner must seek to do what makes sense. Sometimes a fast loan at a high interest rate is practical, and other times a more conservative approach is required. You should be aware of the different options and considerations.

48. Choosing a Lawyer

While it is not advisable that small businesses get themselves into litigations, it will be unavoidable in some cases. In any event, there is a need for legal advice from time to time even without litigations.

The use of a large experienced firm can be expensive, and the use of a low-cost inexperienced lawyer can be expensive, too, in the long run. Depending on the issue at hand, the choice of a lawyer can be routine or strategic. Perhaps an analogy can be made with doctors. A relatively inexpensive general practitioner can be useful at one stage, while an expensive heart surgeon is needed at another.

To get a suitable fit, you may want to draw upon the experience of your contacts; networking can uncover how certain cases were handled. Or, just as good doctors specialize in certain fields, a reputable lawyer or firm will be known for handling certain types of cases.

The balance between affordability and the necessary expertise must be achieved.

Avoid friends and relatives in some cases. The lawyer who is your cousin might be more emotionally caught up in your sacrifices and disappointments over the last ten years than he is with giving good, dispassionate advice. The end result might not be in your interest.

Lucky is the businessman who can make it without expensive and time-consuming court cases.

This might be achieved by developing good negotiation and people skills. Many cases go to litigation needlessly. In some cases, there are provisions for mediation and conflict resolution, and you can check around your area for organizations that do this.

I know someone who had a dispute with a supplier who demanded payment for a product that was ordered but was found to be unnecessary. They had a standoff for a time, and a very thoughtful lawyer suggested they discuss the matter with a certain businessman whom the parties respected. He made them agree to commit to the final decision, whatever it was, and they went ahead, got some fresh ideas about the problem, and saved themselves a lot of time, money, and aggravation.

There is a network and system for the overall area of "alternative dispute resolution," which includes arbitration, conflict resolution, negotiation, mediation, etc. Many cities have these in place, and the Internet can be helpful in locating them, or you can try the local small-business connections, chambers of commerce, legal-aid services, and so forth.

Small-Business Summary

The small business should take steps to avoid litigations as much as possible. This is a big drain on time and money, if only because some issues cannot move forward until legal rulings have been made. However, research and select legal assistance with care so that you make the best efforts at defending your interests if forced to do so.

49. Investing

Of course, every business wants to get to the point where it can have money in "investments." These can be real estate (buying that site for the office upgrade) or stocks, bonds, certificates of deposit, etc.

I have seen people more actively concerned about what kind of return they can make on financial instruments than about their core business. I have also seen situations where government policy made it lucrative to focus on the returns from financial instruments.

In a small business where one person may have to decide and act, where there is much competing information, and where the issues of the business are overwhelming, one cannot afford to lose focus.

I am all for the efficient use of funds. But if you are in a business and the circumstances require your full attention, then you might be in for a surprise when the interest rates on real estate prices and financial instruments fluctuate, and you have to spend your time evaluating market options. Most times, you can do something about the returns from your business but not a lot about the returns on outside investments.

What about the possibility of needing cash at a certain point and having it tied up in a twelve-month instrument? These circumstances are not abnormal and can be optimized, but the entrepreneur should not walk into them blindly, driven simply by interest rates.

The recent spate of the Ponzi schemes and other "investment" scams should be a warning for all to be cautious about diverting their funds into "lucrative" investments.

If it sounds too good to be true, it probably is.

Small-Business Summary

In the first two years or so, investing outside of your business should not be a strong interest. You might see "opportunities" to invest and divert resources to maximize the return on your money, but before you do so, examine your commitment to your business as well as what these opportunities promise. If you tie up funds in alternatives to your business, the business might starve for needed cash.

50. Putting It All Together

The ideas discussed in this book are time-tested; many businesses apply most of them already.

Most business ventures are in fact simple, but not always easy. Let's say you buy cars from a supplier, add a markup, then sell them to your customers. That is easy to do, but many people have failed when trying to do it.

There is an interconnectivity that requires a balancing act.

In business, most decisions you make will have repercussions elsewhere. You price incorrectly or give unnecessary discounts and have to work harder to make up for the revenue targets. Or maybe you refuse to give discounts, and customers take their business elsewhere. You fail to replace poor employees, and you get burned out trying to make up for what they should be doing. Or you wait in vain to get the perfect employee and operate ineffectively.

Most experiences suggest that commitment and discipline best assure success.

Business, at any stage, is a process. It should not be an end in itself; otherwise, it will stagnate. One business can stay a small "mom-and-pop" operation, while another can grow to become a global force. And both can be successful.

There is nothing intrinsically wrong with staying small, but there should be a conscious effort to understand what is happening and decide how you want things to be.

Evolve to suit your aspirations and the times.

Keep yourself and your staff abreast of developments that affect the business. Be open to learning and applying new thinking and new ways.

How can you grow if you don't adopt new ideas or learn about new things in business, sales, and marketing? How can you expect to advance to higher levels if you stop investing in your knowledge?

Some aspects of business are unsavory and can get ignored or overlooked.

Once you get yourself thinking about some things, other ideas will emerge, and you will get answers to your specific situations.

I will close with a summary of how one could approach the start-up of a business with some very simple perspectives. From these eleven steps, one can easily be guided into action.

Small-Business Start-Up (Practical Exercises)

1. **Assess talents.** What skills, interests, hobbies, or talents can you identify?
   - What things bug you (for example, containers used by a store are too small/large)?
   - What product or service is not fulfilling needs (for example, the grocery is often out of some types of vegetables, fruits, etc.)?
   - What service takes too long and why (for example, it takes the mechanic too long to repair cars)?
   - What bad experience presents an opportunity (for example, your father got locked out of his house at midnight and could not find a locksmith)?
   - What are some seasonal demands (for example, what your friends need for the long summer break)?
   - What do you notice people have to do but dislike doing (for example, washing their cars themselves, going shopping for themselves, walking their pets, etc.)?
   - What do you notice you do better than most people (for example, a guy who was an underachiever in most areas of life found he had special skills for hunting birds and became a professional hunting guide then wrote a book about hunting)?
   - If you are good at some subjects, you can develop a homework module, showing how to deal with certain situations, problems, and challenges associated with some subjects. Tips and hints about them can evolve into useful publications.
2. **Consider how the business will operate.** Some can start informally without registration, but those involving the food and health industries, for example, might require varying approvals and licenses to operate.
3. **Define your business.** Identify your passions, strengths, and weaknesses, and use this knowledge to determine your small-business niche (area of greatest opportunity), products, and/or service.

4. **Define your target market.** Understand your target market needs, how to spot capable competitors within your niche, and how to research and document the demographics, expected growth, and other important characteristics of your target market.
5. **Document your business intentions in terms of a careful plan.** This might be necessary for bankers or others giving a loan. Include a marketing plan and cash flow statement.
6. **Deal with your fears and frustrations.** What are the likely emotions that will be creeping into your daily experiences?
7. **Finance your business.** Many small businesses require start-up capital. Public or private sources are possible. Private sources usually have a profit motive, and public sources (government and aid/donating bodies) are options.
8. **Market your business.** The most important factor in the success of any small business is the cultivation of relationships with satisfied clients. Use a step-by-step guide to earning reliable revenue from repeat customers. Especially for your team-members who have not yet bought into your system, provide a written process that details how to follow up with customers for repeat business, up-sell, cross-sell, and upgrade initiatives.
9. **Network and build relationships.** Realize that who you know is important. Try to build mutually beneficial relationships. Find a sound, systematic tool or approach. Aim for *mutually* beneficial relationships so that others grow as you grow! Examples are: client base sharing or commissions on referrals.
10. **Provide products/services.**
    - Designing, submitting, and managing proposals to clients and prospects
    - Getting orders
    - Invoicing and delivering
    - Getting paid
    - Customer service
11. **Maintain a client base.** Cultivate solid and successful relationships with satisfied customers. Repeat business is key to growth and progress.

Above all, have some fun!

INDEX

www.ingramcontent.com/pod-product-compliance
Lightning Source LLC
Chambersburg PA
CBHW051525170526
45165CB00002B/612
* 9 7 8 1 4 3 9 2 6 8 3 1 5 *